FEMINISM and BEYOND

A Theological Reflection for the Next Aeon

By

Loretta Dornisch

authorHOUSE

1663 LIBERTY DRIVE, SUITE 200
BLOOMINGTON, INDIANA 47403
(800) 839-8640
www.authorhouse.com

First published by AuthorHouse 07/29/04

ISBN: 1-4184-3434-5 (e)
ISBN: 1-4184-3433-7 (sc)

Library of Congress Control Number: 2004093397

Printed in the United States of America
Bloomington, Indiana

This book is printed on acid-free paper.

TABLE OF CONTENTS

CHAPTER I:
WHAT IS THEOLOGICAL REFLECTION?

Chapter One:
What Is Theological Reflection?

What is theological reflection? What is happening in our worlds today? What do we think about the "gods" of our childhood? How does this relate to any of the forms of feminism which sprouted up in the last decades of the twentieth century? Exploring these questions in a dialectic of world views may shed light on what is happening in these times of cultural earthquakes and the explosion of new ways of viewing our universe.

Plato was perhaps the first to use the word "theology" to indicate thoughts or meaning-statements about the gods. For Plato in the fourth century BCE the gods were the pantheon handed down in tradition to explain natural events and historical or human events. These had been described in Greek mythology at least from the time of Homer in the tenth century BCE. By the time of Plato, the stories of the gods were unreal to the educated persons with whom he interacted. This was an age in which their world view was recognized as naive and a new world view was forming.

In many ways, this transition characterizes the experience of many cultures and persons today. The stories and the myths, the configurations of their world views, are shifting mightily. Persons are disillusioned. Their worlds fall apart. In some cases they search for new arrangements of meaning. New languages, new stories, even new religions, or religions new to them, provide a new way of thinking about their lives. They convert from Catholicism to Buddhism, or from a Baptist tradition to Islam, or from secularism to Judaism. A structure new to them gives new community, new meaning, and new hope. This is happening, not only to individuals, but also to small and large communities, to whole churches or temples, and even to regional or national groups.

Where does feminism fit into these transitions? What do we mean by feminism? Is feminism related to theological reflection? For the moment, I will define feminism in the words of Mary Ann Zimmer:

> Feminism is a complex movement with many branches and streams.[1] Most feminists, though, would agree with the definition of the feminist project as it is laid out by bell hooks. Feminism, hooks asserts, can best be defined as "the struggle to end sexist oppression."[2]

The struggle of women to end sexist oppression is an integral and ongoing part of these world shaking transitions. Even those women who oppose feminism as they know it are involved in the struggle for justice. Women in India who gather together and embrace the trees so they cannot be cut down and destroy their environment are part of this struggle. Women in Albania who walk in protest raising loaves of bread to indicate their needs are part of this struggle. Women in Central America who work to build a three room school for their children's education may not know the word feminism, but they know the struggle.

Feminism is related by choice or by default to theological reflection.

In North America many Christian women move from traditional Christianity with its patriarchal structures, first to a reaction against these structures, and then to a search for the earth goddess and then to the goddess within. In the cultural and political movements of Guatemala, El Salvador, and other Central American nations, women grow through their reflections on the Bible and through their recognition of oppression to a new sense of themselves as persons, as women. They become leaders. They learn to work in solidarity. They name a God who calls them from oppression to an exodus into human dignity.

With the help of others, Buddhist nuns with much difficulty escape the oppressions of the restrictions in Tibet and escape to India. Supported by Indians, Buddhists, and North Americans, they are seeking education and the environment in which to practice their traditional faiths. Korean women are recognizing how they have been used as economic slaves and are clamoring for dignity as they reclaim the support of their indigenous religious beliefs. Caribbean women in the islands as well as in south Florida are rediscovering qualities of their voodoo and African roots which give them strength to resist white or black oppression.

Theological reflection, reflection on the meaning of God or gods, reflection on the symbols which comprise our world views, reflection on our relationship with nature, with our histories or herstories, with all the human events of which we are part, and indeed with the cosmos, open up a way perhaps to understand, and to move the critique to developments of the twenty-first century and perhaps of a new aeon. Plato as well as many of the biblical writers were familiar with the concept of a succession of aeons, of ages, of worlds. Of some aeons in the past we have little or no knowledge. Those in the future we can only speculate about. But the concept can open our minds to new directions, to new ways of thinking, and to the possibilities of hope.

CHAPTER II:

FEMINISM IN THE TWENTY-FIRST CENTURY

Chapter Two:

Feminism in the 21st Century

Who are the women of the 21st century?

In China many of those women do not exist, either because they were not allowed to develop in the womb or because they were allowed to die as girl children. Statistically, women should be close to 50% of Chinese people. Since the last century, the percentage is closer to 40%. What are their gifts which never had the opportunity to develop? What is the wisdom of which the 21st century is deprived?

In El Salvador or Guatemala the women are the children or grandchildren of the heroes or survivors of the revolutions and civil wars. They perhaps grew up in a village populated mostly by women because many of the men "were disappeared." As children they may have tagged along as their mothers engaged in the exhumation of bodies buried in mass graves. Perhaps they were there when a scarf or ribbon helped identify the body of a sibling. They learned courage as they breathed the air.

In Africa the women of the 21st century are those who are newly teaching African Studies in community colleges or universities. Their degrees may be from Zurich or New York. But other women in Africa may walk the famine road knowing that their children will not survive.

Many of these women will not know the term "feminism," but they will know well their oppression as women and their struggles for justice or even for survival.

> With a little bit of common sense, today no one would dare deny that women make up more than 50 percent of the Latin American population, that most of these women live in impoverished conditions, that as a social group, exploited men share in a relation of domination over women, and that it

continues to be true that the great majority of Latin American women are still "the oppressed among the oppressed."[3]

In North America, on the other hand, most women do not face famine. Some, however, still face hunger, still struggle against oppression, whether in the home, in the workplace, or in the racist and sexist systems of which they are part.

A few women in each continent have become conscious that one of the sources of systemic injustice is sexism, and that naming the problem is to name the need for feminism.

The feminist proposal is oriented toward a "utopia" better defined now by what we do not want than by what we do know. Perhaps it cannot be in any other way since the very social practices that we are creating are those that are prefiguring the content of new forms of accomplishments, of new concepts...In the presence of this reality, it is not only necessary to revise our social practices and the [theoretical] assumptions that we weave around them. We must also raise the question of a discourse which can crystallize concepts and which can force us to act according to a model (however libertarian and democratic it may be, it is still a model) without rescuing the contradictions of the process. We must also recognize that "fortunately" not everything is included in our proposal. Instead, its content is being profiled and nourished on the basis of our difficulties, doubts, pursuits, joys, frustrations, errors and our discussions, in short [our] vital social practices, which allows us to pave the way while we are building it.[4]

Among the women naming the feminist struggle are secular women with no religious traditions or with traditions they have rejected as patriarchal and therefore oppressive. But there are also women who remain within their religious traditions and yet recognize the systemic discrimination through which they walk. Some of these are women theologians, biblical scholars, or atheists. They have been trained in the largely patriarchal universities, seminaries, or theological schools, but their consciousness has reached a level in which they are in tension;

at the same time, they can critique the patriarchal content and methodologies through which they have passed.[5]

What are the challenges in the 21st century for feminism? What are the challenges for women whether they know or relate to the word "feminism"?

BODY

The basic challenge for women around the globe is Body, their bodies and the bodies of their children. What is my body? It is the miracle given to me in time and place. A strange combination of chemicals gathers into a genetic configuration. The embryo grows in my Mother's womb and emerges as the person I am becoming. Genes, nutrition, nurturing, choices continue to form the body of my person until I become the body I am today.

If we are fortunate to have parents with healthy genes, we have a good start. If, in addition, they or their surrogates show us love and feed us properly, we add a positive spin towards health. As we grow older, we assume more responsibility for the choices we make. Our food choices, exercise, the persons we associate with, what we do with our education,--all affect our bodies.

But for many women today there are other factors which are changing women's bodies, affecting their future, and the future of the globe. First may come to mind the pictures of women in Africa enduring famine or war or both. Their bodies, more than lean, walk towards an unknown future, often carrying or pulling along their children. Medical workers in villages or refugee camps see the clear signs of malnutrition or parasites. Even if they had the best of medical care, the future would probably not seem friendly. They walk in the world of lamentation, and yet most will struggle on to whatever hope they can find.

In all worlds across the economic strata, many girls and women embody abuse and violence that have leached their sufferings into their minds, emotions, hearts, and wills. Any woman who has not suffered such abuses usualiy knows someone who has, or else she walks in denial. The woman who hears the story of abuse feels a ripple in her own body which empathizes with the violation. No woman, no child is safe as long as abuse is allowed to go on.

Violence and abuse may thrive in the environment of alcohol and drugs, but the combination takes new virulent forms when the child in the womb or the new born is a crack baby. Some abuses of alcohol and drugs perpetrated by the pregnant woman may not be evident as transferred until the child is ten or eleven years old. The body has read its program in the womb and the program is acted out like a time bomb many years later.

SPIRIT

It is woman's spirit which created the pre-historic, as well as the continuing tradition of the earth goddess, who at the same time is often the cosmic goddess or spirit of the universe.

Those people close to the earth know that the earth and the air are the sources of all life. The earth is the substance from which we see the grasses and flowers emerge. Women close to the earth have often brought forth their children on that earth. Some women working on *fincas* in Central America or on farms in China may still do that today. And this happens in the United States as well, not only on the land, but sometimes on the concrete of our cities as well.

What is the air? Although we may analyze it, it has always stood as symbol for the cosmos, for the mysterious force of the universe, which somehow gives life. The Hebrews and other peoples recognized this. The Hebrew word for wind is *ruah*, spirit, including winds of the universe, but also the breath which fills the lungs of each child who is born. This is the same wind which fills the lungs of large mammals, of giraffes, and of minuscule animals of the forest or the jungle. In their own way, plants also breathe this *ruah*, this wind, this air. Insofar as they are alive, these persons, these animals, these plants are in-spirited.

A woman who brings forth a child brings forth body and spirit. The Hebrew language tradition treasures this by comparing the potter's bringing forth of a pot from clay to the woman's bringing forth of a child. The name for the midwife's seat is the same name as the potter's seat, close to the earth, bringing forth from the earth.

Spirit, *ruah*, on the other hand, is the mysterious life-force of the universe. Unless the child's lungs fill with this precious air, the child does not live. If a person has the air "knocked out of her," her life is threatened. Sometimes a person needs mouth to mouth resuscitation. At such a moment, one human being transfers the breath, the spirit, from herself to another. We say that someone gave out her last breath. We hold a mirror to a dying person's mouth to see if any breathing continues.

The Gospels tell us: Jesus gave up his spirit, breathed out his spirit. The Gospel word which translates *ruah* is *pneuma*. We think of pneumatic tires, pneumonia, and other cognates. These words describe not only physical realities, but also symbolic levels of life which transcend the physical.

We recognize in some persons a great spirit. It is the force of a great personality, but often it also defies physical limitations. Gandhi, often thin and physically weak, overflowed with spirit. Another example is Mother Teresa, so inspirited she was a force to be reckoned with on a global scale. In a similar way, Dorothy Day's spirit still lives in some of the social justice traditions of the United States.

We recognize this embodied but transcending spirit when someone comes into a room and the room is transformed from lifelessness to life. Jesus must have been this kind of person. He had this kind of spirit. Christians name this a holy spirit, a Holy Spirit, the spirit of Jesus, the spirit of the Father and Mother of Jesus.

This spirit in the Hebrew tradition is also the spirit of wisdom. Just as *ruah* is a feminine word, so also is *sophia*. Each is personified as woman. *Sophia* is gift. She is intelligent and holy. She reveals herself in many ways. She is free. She loves what is good. She is kind and a friend of humanity. She is dependable. She is a breath of God's power. She is a reflection of everlasting light, a mirror of God's action. She is more beautiful than the sun and all constellations. She is better than light itself. (See the Wisdom of Solomon 7:22-29).

But, although this spirit, this wisdom-life is universal, and we all partake of it, nevertheless it is also unique to each individual. Each life is unique. Not only is the body of each identical twin unique, but even the spirit of each Siamese twin. Though joined in body, each spirit is unique. Even if we can clone ourselves in the future, each clone will have a unique spirit.

When Jesus gave forth his spirit, he gave his life force, but each of us receives the spirit and transforms the life in our own unique way.

So what is a human life? Embodied spirit. Unique. Connected to the universe. You. Me. Others.

ACTION

A person, however, is not static. She moves. She acts. In its roots, the word *act* means *to drive* or *to do.*[6] Dylan Thomas speaks of the "force that drives." In a person's story, the action is the driving force. It is that which pushes the characters or persons to do what they do, to engage in the conflicts in which they find themselves, to make the decisions which they are called to make, or which they refuse to make. It is this driving force which creates the plots of their lives.

In each human life, the person is the *protagonist,* the hero or anti-hero in her story. Protagonist is an interesting word in this context. *Proto* means first. By reason of our being the body/spirit which we are, we are *proto* in our story. It cannot be otherwise, even though we may be called or may choose to give our life

21

for another. *Agon* is the struggle, the *agony* in the sense of the struggle of life. Luke tells of Jesus on the Mount of Olives, "And being in an *agony* he prayed more earnestly" (Lk 22:44). His agony was not just that moment, but the whole struggle of his existence, his struggle to fulfill the will of his Father, his struggle to become the person he chose to be.

Who is the antagonist in our life story? Who is struggling against the becoming of ourselves? It is anyone or any persons who militate against our becoming the fully human beings we are called to be. Sometimes "we are our own worst enemies." That is, the chief antagonist is within ourselves. "I cannot even understand my own actions. I do not do what I want to do but what I hate" (Rom 7:15).

Often, of course, the antagonists are other persons, whether family, friends, or outsiders. For whatever reason, they are sometimes in conflict with our process of becoming human, of becoming fully ourselves. One of the insightful findings of contemporary theology is that often the antagonist is not so much a person or persons, but the structures created by individuals or groups of persons which take on personalities of their own, and which often are structurally dehumanizing. These structures may be the governmental bureaucracy which transforms persons into numbers in a welfare line. They may be family situations which breed violence through child abuse or other kinds of manipulation. They may be church structures which subordinate the person to the preservation of the *status quo*. Permeating most other structures is the prevalent one of the dollar sign, of the economic systems which too often fight the process of humanization. These may include the local store purveying the wares made by oppressed people working in Mexico. They include many aspects of international economy, including the supra-nationals as the new global corporations or the new religions.

The persons and structures mentioned above as *antagonists* may, however, in a given story, not be antagonists at all, but persons and structures which help or work *with* the protagonist in her struggle. Then they are not antagonists, but assistants in the process of becoming human. A liberating family, a community, or a society can be gift in furthering the action of the story. Not only that, but the antagonist may also be transformed into friend and helper in the protagonist's struggle. With the help of counseling and grace, a family subject to violence and manipulation can move to growth enhancing relationships of struggling together.

The life stories of Dorothy Day or Rigoberta Menchu write in large letters the agony, the humanization process, the struggle to transform themselves, others, and structures into life-creating parts of the human story. Their successes, even when minimal, even when communicated through powerlessness, even when communicated through the gift of their lives, are what create hope in our world.

The action or plot of each of our stories has a particular setting, a particular time and place. Maya Angelou speaks out of the particular time and place of her birth, her journey, her experience. Her genes, her choices, her actions become embodied in the writing of her poetry, in the speaking of her truth.

In the spirit of that kind of truth, feminists grow in consciousness as they ask what are the lines of the struggles in which they are engaged? Where is the focus in which they find themselves protagonist? Who or what, or what systems are the antagonist? What is the action they must take in order to become the fully human persons they can be? Where do their struggles intersect with the struggles of other women?

MOVEMENT

Movement is development. It is another way of looking at plot or action. It implies a change in position. Each life story unfolds in a major plot line. The rhythm is fast or slow, angular or smooth. It is composed of a series of starts and stops, or it is as regular as the change of summer into fall. The movement may be simple or complex, the plot line uncluttered or interwoven with many sub-plots. Whatever the rhythm of the movement, there are patterns that sometimes may be read ahead of time, but which, more often, are perceived only afterward as configurations of a life story or as a dance unfolded with organic rhythm, line, and space.

General patterns supplied by disciplines, heroes, or cultures may be helpful in understanding the movement and in freeing it to its unique potential. Patterns described by psychologists provide insight for some of the developmental tasks which challenge us as human beings. Great heroes--whether our grandmother, our mother, our spouse or significant other, a teacher, a Sojourner

Truth, a Rigoberta Menchu--show us how to live our lives. Our pattern is not the same as theirs, but the configurations are similar.

Culture sets before us patterns that are presumed to be "natural," but which often go unexamined, and which may be liberating or oppressive. These vary from the patterns provided by a work ethic, a sports metaphor, or a Christian saying, "See how they love one another." Whatever the patterns, the movement involves moments of insight, decision, choice, action, and the consequences which flow from these moments and which also lead to new insights and decisions.

The insights of early women leaders in developing countries around the world lead to decisions for many women. These decisions flow into choices, actions, and consequences which for some lead to death, for others to land reform, and for still others to reactionary solidification in establishment structures.

WORDS AND SYMBOLS

You may remember the moment in the story of Helen Keller when she was freed for language by matching a word to experience. As the water flowed over her hands, she finally understood her teacher, and was able to cry "Water!" She named and she knew. The word creates new worlds of relationship, of meaning. It makes poetry of the chaotic. It gives interpretation to unformed experience. Such words woven together become myths, narratives of meaning or non-meaning. They give order to the chaos through an interpretation which creates meaning, or they interpret the chaos in an anti-story of non-meaning. We find such, for example, in a play by Becket, *Waiting for Godot.* In human life, story and anti-story meet at the edge of experience. Thus our words fall short of the mystery and absurdity which are the components of human life. They often dance in paradox.

Reflecting the story of our lives, our words, narratives, and symbols are constantly in motion. They are constantly forming and reforming. Like the cells in a body, they group and regroup. They disorient and then reorient. They describe, then break the horizons of the description in order to redescribe in the light of new experience. They are partners with the icons we paint, with the images, the dances, the architecture, and the music which weave together the stories of our lives.

Toni Morrison's novels are good examples of the power of word and symbols to create a narrative that textures meaning out of chaos. Such images transform a tumble of worlds into hope. No wonder such novels speak to women. They help them name their oppressions and at the same time name the possibilities of transformation and freedom. So we see the challenges as we examine the structures of Body, Spirit, Action, Movement, Words and Symbols. We move next to another framework as foundation for dialectic.

CHAPTER III:

FEMINIST INTERPRETATION AND OTHER TRADITIONS: A FRAMEWORK FOR ANALYSIS

Chapter Three:

Feminist Interpretation and Other Traditions: A Framework for Analysis

What can feminist interpretations learn from other traditions?

What can other traditions learn from feminist interpretations?

These two questions are needed today. Too often feminist thought and thought in other traditions are polarized. Proponents build walls around their citadels. They are afraid, or at least defensive, often basing their position on negative experience. Perhaps they have tried to communicate and were met with rejection, scorn, or worse. The temptation, then, is to cease efforts to interact, to presume bad will on the part of the other, and henceforth to dialogue only within the group. Prejudice is often the outcome, as well as misunderstanding.

Principles for Discourse

In his book *Method in Theology*, Bernard Lonergan lays out some principles which can be helpful in addressing the challenges of discourse and interpretation.[7] He describes eight functional specialties in theological method. The language and basic meanings can be appropriated to give us a framework for feminist studies in themselves and in connection with other studies.[8]

The eight functional specialties are : research, interpretation, history, dialectic, foundations, doctrines, systematics, and communications. In a way, depending on the discipline or experience from which they have come, women scholars are plunged into one or several of these, sometimes without acknowledging or even being conscious of their methods.

Research involves the compilation of data. Those scholars who have discovered texts and perhaps have published women's slave narratives, women's journals or poetry provide texts and data for new understanding of women's experience. The multiplication of accounts of Third World women's experience, such as those of Rigoberta Menchu, provide raw material for reassessing women's conditions. Those who chronicle enslavement of women in our time, or who give an indication of how widespread tourist prostitution is, or who estimate the number of abortions and deaths of girl children, provide data which is shocking to the reader and which cries out for interpretation.

Following the tradition of literary studies, Lonergan divides *Interpretation* into "hermeneutics" and "exegesis" (153). "Hermeneutics" consists of principles of interpretation and "exegesis" is the application of the principles to a particular task or event. Elisabeth Schlussler-Fiorenza engaged in both when she wrote *In Memory of Her*[9]. While basically following generally accepted principles of interpretation and methods of exegesis, Fiorenza nevertheless asked new questions of some New Testament texts. New questions called for new ways of looking at the texts, at the principles of interpretation, and new ways of applying those principles to exegetical work. Few could fault Fiorenza on her methods and pursuits, but many in the more traditional modes refused to consider her questions seriously, or to recognize her new insights. However, many, especially women scholars, recognized a new breakthrough, an opening to a new way of thinking. A deluge of new studies followed and continue. Indeed, a new "differentiation of consciousness" (302ff) has arrived on the scene.

Women biblical scholars from Africa bring cultural backgrounds which add new directions for interpretation. In interpreting the role of Joseph in the infancy narrative, for example, one woman emphasizes Joseph's compassion and voices the wish that African men might be as compassionate as Joseph.

Women in base communities of Central America interpret anew the Exodus stories as dynamic and contemporary in their own political and economic situations. More than one see the crucifixion and resurrection of Jesus as contemporary and corporate. "If you do not help us to life, then Jesus is still dead in the tomb. If you help us to life, Jesus' resurrection is reality." (Paraphrased from Maria Sorran. Talk given at Edgewood College, Madison, Wisconsin, April 19, 1998. After enduring the horrors of war in her country, Maria became an elected delegate from her district to the National Assembly of El Salvador. Her face beams the hope of resurrection.)

One North American, after returning from meeting with the people of El Salvador and hearing their stories, came to a new realization as he was singing the Passion during Holy Week Service. This passion-crucifixion was not just about Jesus or a liturgical ritual. This text is about the passion-crucifixion of the people of El Salvador and such people wherever they may be. So interpretation and exegesis are changing as we acknowledge the diversity of our cultural and political worlds.

In *History* human beings tell their stories. If a person tells her own story, we call it autobiography. If we tell the story of someone else, we call it biography. If we tell the story of a group, a community, or a nation, we may call it "history" in the broad sense (Lonergan 182 ff.), but the writing of history is recognized as much more suspect than it used to be.

"History" depends not only on what data are gathered, what exegesis and interpretation are applied to that data, but especially on what questions are asked of the data. For example, most of western "history," including the "history" of Christianity, was written by men, based on data compiled from their man-related experiences, and interpreted from those perspectives. Approximately half the population for two thousand years were women, so half the experience was that of women, but we have very little data and very little history from all those experiences. More recently, women scholars are researching women such as Perpetua, Monica, Hildegard of Bingen, Clare of Assisi, and Catherine of Siena. There are new translations, new publications, new "herstories." Scholars are also reading "between the lines" of male records and deconstructing or reconstructing the herstory of women's lives. But the scarcity of materials is shocking.

What can be said of western history is probably more true of African, Asian, and Latin American history, literature and theology. Kyung[10] tells of studying all male theologians, mostly German, in her college work in Korea, and only gradually realizing as she continued her studies in New York how biased her education was. Not only had she not learned about any women writers, but she had ignored the women's stories and traditions in her own country. A major conversion and differentiation of consciousness was required before she could recognize her bias and reclaim her women's tradition. A similar journey takes place in theological schools or colleges in every continent.

The fourth of the functional specialties is *Dialectic.* The etymology of the word suggests reading one view against another or in contrast to another. *Lect* refers to reading and *dia* against or across. Lonergan sees all dialectic related to conflicts (235ff). He lists religious sources, traditions, authoritative pronouncements, but also contradictory orientations of research, interpretations, and histories. He links the problems to contradictory evaluations, horizons, doctrines, systems, and policies. He argues that such contradictions are only overcome by conversions.

What does he mean by conversion? A conversion is a turning with. One's vision is limited by one's horizon, the boundary of what one sees, or one's vision. "Differences in horizon may be complementary, or genetic, or dialectical" (236). Persons live in different worlds by reason of heredity, career, or cultural background. These different worlds may be understood as complementary and appropriate or as threatening. Women and men may even understand their differences as complementary or as opposed.

Why do these horizons differ? Why are world views contradictory? There are many examples. Horizons which differ genetically affect developmental stages. Most American young women are culturally interested in traditional marriages. They are not usually open to understand or acknowledge systemic sexism. On the other hand, an additional ten or twenty years of experience raise questions which make them able to see the cultural sexism which is related to invisible ceilings against promotion in business, sexism which tolerates or excuses rape or abuse, sexism which often puts double expectations on women, sexism which denies access to religious leadership or ordination.

"Horizons may be opposed dialectically" (236). For Lonergan, such horizons are polarized. For example, if church authorities understand as "good" the defense of a tradition which opens ordination only to men, then such a horizon understands the opposite, opening ordination to women, as evil.

What for one is good, for another is evil. Each may have some awareness of the other and so each in a manner may include the other. But such inclusion is also negation and rejection. For the other's horizon, at least in part, is attributed to wishful thinking, to an acceptance of myth, to ignorance or fallacy, to blindness or illusion, to backwardness or immaturity, to infidelity, to bad will, to a refusal of God's grace. Such a rejection of the other may be passionate, and then the suggestion that openness is desirable will make one furious. But again rejection may have the firmness of ice without any trace of passion or even any show of feeling, except perhaps a wan smile (236-237).

It is possible, however, to move from one horizon to another, whether by an enlargement, a deepening, or even by a reversal (237). Such a reversal Lonergan calls a conversion, whether intellectual, moral, or religious. The first committee appointed by the Vatican to research scriptural foundations related to women's ordination, approached the task with appropriate scriptural tools and scholarly openness. Study and dialogue led to their conclusion that there are no scriptural bases opposed to women's ordination. When their report was presented to Vatican authorities, it was rejected because the authoritative horizon had no place for the possibility of women's ordination. A new commission was later constituted with a presumed agenda of different findings. Some male priests who during the time of rising consciousness about sexism went through intellectual, moral, and/or religious conversions, felt such attacks on their integrity that they felt obliged to leave the official priesthood.

Another philosopher, Paul Ricoeur, who calls himself a philosopher of faith, offers a model different from Lonergan's, a model of convergence. Provided there is a willingness to enter into sincere dialogue, opposed roads or viewpoints may be seen as possible of convergence. Like spokes in a wheel, the closer they come to a center (which may be thought of as truth), the closer they come to each other.

The dialectic, however applies to the other functional specialties as well. Research and the gathering of data continue in learned ways, until the possibility of a new horizon emerges. Among others, astronomers, astro-physicists, and biologists have experienced a century of constantly expanding horizons. They provide new paradigms of chaos and cosmic patterns. Some women find the paradigms exciting, not only as paradigms, but because they show new ways of thinking and new possibilities for change.

Something similar is true of interpretation. Putting one way of interpreting against another opens up new knowledge. Pushing the dialectic to full reversal shakes assumed ways of perceiving. Studying some native American societies which are matrilineal opens up new ways of interpreting data.

The effect of the dialectic is perhaps most obvious when we apply it to history. French historians and historiographers have used new structures as well as new data to rewrite medieval history from the point of view of peasant life. To some degree, Crossan and other biblical scholars use new sociological models to rewrite the gospels and the story of Jesus.

Likewise, as they find new resources in epistemology, the study of knowledge, or ways of knowing, women engage in a dialectic with traditional texts. They bring new interpretation to the data, which makes them look for new data. They re-write history from new perspectives.

Lonergan then looks at what he calls *Foundations*.

> At its real root, then, foundations occurs on the fourth level of human consciousness, on the level of deliberation, evaluation, decision. It is a decision about whom and what you are for and, again, whom and what you are against. It is a decision illuminated by the manifold possibilities exhibited in dialectic. It is a fully conscious decision about one's horizon, one's outlook, one's world view. It deliberately selects the frame-work, in which doctrines have their meaning, in which systematics reconciles, in which communications are effective.[11]

The above describes the experience of many women. As their consciousness of exclusion, of the use of skewed data, of patriarchal interpretations, of biased history grew, so did their acknowledgment of the value of dialectic. They claimed their own experience. They validated their insights through comparison with other women, other disciplines, or other traditions. Their "foundations were shaken" (Tillich). Conversion to different or enlarged horizons in some cases made previous foundations suspect, or even to be rejected. For some women in the Roman Catholic tradition, Eucharist which is linked only to male authority and patriarchal ritual was recognized as a contradiction of the good news of love, a contradiction of "love your neighbor as yourself," and a deviance from Paul's insight: "In Christ there is neither Jew nor gentile, male and female. All are one in Christ" (Gal 3:28).

As the foundation this represents is questioned, so are other aspects of the foundation, and indeed the foundations themselves. These may involve hierarchy, patriarchy, injustice, and oppression. New foundations are called for. One theoretical possibility is the reworking of a patriarchal church into a just society which is inclusive. For many this is seen as hopeless, so they move to foundations in goddess religions, in Christian traditions perceived as more inclusive, to Buddhism, or to a secularized world view related to their positive experience.

Often this means departing from family, friends, sexual partners, husbands, wives, children. They feel their integrity is at stake.

Others move to an emphasis on interiority, or transcendence, or they despair of finding or creating foundations, or perhaps they move to action for action's sake. We are reminded of the earlier example of Schweitzer who gave up on the academic or accepted intellectual and religious foundations of his world in Germany and spent the rest of his life doing medical work in Africa. Many women have followed similar courses, some equally dramatic, some less dramatic.

The challenge for women is to find or build new foundations. What can build the new foundations for their lives? Some find resources in a new relationship of love, or in a community which represents unconditional love. Some find foundations for their lives in a religious setting, whether church, synagogue, or temple. Others discover anew a commitment to gospel values and to the example of Jesus as a model of unconditional love which moves through teaching and healing to daily crucifixion and resurrection. Foundations are always threatened. Many other world views raise contradictions. Brokenness appears every morning. Sometimes one is reduced to putting the finger in the dike and hoping the dike holds. Renewal takes effort and energy and structures to make it happen. Friends and community members can help but this kind of responsibility often lies with the individual. Relying on grace, praying for the gift becomes a letting go which may lead to, if not a new foundation, a river that takes its place.

The word *Doctrines* means teachings. For most feminists, the word is objectionable because it suggests patriarchy and authoritarianism which they reject. However, it is sometimes easy to fall into a position similar to the one we reject.

What teachings do feminists espouse? It depends, of course, on the world view of the feminists involved. Especially in the United States it is interesting to see how some feminists by rejecting patriarchy become equally dogmatic espousing anti-patriarchy as sometimes anti-male. Some males are offended by "male-bashing." By reason of using inclusive language, these persons eliminate the word "father" from texts and rituals. Under the illusion that "father" automatically connotes patriarchy and oppression, they formulate "doctrinal" or "teaching" positions that are not only doctrinal but dogmatic. In the area of theology, Lonergan distinguishes the two:

> Dogmatic theology is classicist. It tends to take it for granted that on each issue there is one and only one true proposition. It is out to determine which are the unique propositions that are true. In contrast, doctrinal theology is historically-minded. It knows that the meaning of a proposition becomes determinate only within a context. It knows that contexts vary with the varying brands of common sense, with the evolution of cultures, with the differentiations of human consciousness, and with the presence or absence of intellectual, moral, and religious conversion. In consequence, it distinguished between the religious apprehension of a doctrine and the theological apprehension of the same doctrine. The religious apprehension is through the context of one's own brand of common sense, of one's own evolving culture, of one's undifferentiation or differentiation of consciousness, of one's own unceasing efforts to attain intellectual,

moral, and religious conversion. In contrast, the theological apprehension of doctrines is historical and dialectical. It is historical inasmuch as it grasps the many different contexts in which the same doctrine was expressed in different manners. It is dialectical inasmuch as it discerns the difference between positions and counter-positions and seeks to develop the positions and to reverse the counter-positions.[12]

By ignoring the context and presuming consensus in changing "father" to "god" or "God," some feminists distort the texts and reveal a naiveté in the use, not only of the word "father," but also of the word "God." They do not recognize the latter as rooted in an Old English word indicating a Norse god. Substituting "God" for "father" chooses Nordic, anti-Christian mythology over a familial relationship common to Jesus and all of human kind. If persons have bad experiences of their own fathers, it is understandable that the persons will have difficulty with the term. But the biblical word used by Jesus is precisely not biological. It is a term rich in intimacy, not authoritarian, but indicating a peer relationship. "The father and I are one" (John

10:30). The term is metaphor for the one who is immanent but also transcendent. In "Fatherhood: From Phantasm to Symbol,"[13] Ricoeur makes it clear that to identify Jesus' use or a theological use of "father" with a biological relationship is to misunderstand language and to distort language into idolatry.

In historical context, as well as in the biblical and theological traditions, it is entirely appropriate to speak of the immanent-transcendent as mother, as Hildegard and Julian did in the middle ages. But, again, we are not speaking of biology. We also need to articulate "Motherhood: From Phantasm to Symbol." There is no question that the biological is foundational for the concept, but the set of images and concepts are not just biological. Equally necessary is to understand that we must go beyond the "godness" of God and beyond the "goddessness" of God.

For those who see the term "father" as oppressive, it is the biblical tradition which has precisely provided the way of claiming fatherhood and motherhood as beyond the biological experience. To pretend that fatherhood and motherhood are unnecessary to human experience is not only to ignore the realities of the human condition, but also to deprive the persons involved of some of the most basic metaphors and concepts which our language supplies.

Something similar may be said of those feminists who dogmatically exclude the tradition of calling Jesus or God by the title "Lord." They dogmatically teach that the word is oppressive and patriarchal. They are unable to separate its connotation from the experience associated with males.

Although the word often suggests dominance, the word itself is from the Old English *hlafweard*, which means "keeper of the bread," the one who provides for bread and other necessities. It implies that no human being is autonomous, but is in community. The universe is a given, and a gift. "Life" is a gift. "Bread" or whatever maintains life is a gift. To give a face to the giver of this creation, this universe, this bread, is to humanize an otherwise non-human world. To claim a false independence of the universe is arrogant, to say the least. Unfortunately, it is also to throw out a tradition which humanizes and makes intimate the God-experience.

The early Christians were faced with similar language problems. The Hebrew names for God included Yahweh, El-Elohim, Adonai, and Shaddai.[14] The names were used for the known-unknown, the God of their fathers and mothers. Yet each was culturally conditioned. Their most insightful name Yahweh, the tetramaton YHWH, is probably an appropriation from an Egyptian concept associated with the sun, "the one who is becoming." Elohim is actually plural, "the gods," used ungrammatically to our way of thinking to name the one God of the Hebrews. Adonai suggests "Lord" in the familial sense of mutual relationship. Shaddai is the appropriation of the anthropomorphic and nature "Storm God." Those translating these into Greek, for the most part chose the Greek word *kyrie*, a generic, personal, and less anthropomorphic allusion to nature god contexts. From the Septuagint, the translation of the Hebrew Bible into Greek, the New Testament writers conflated the term not only with their understanding of the "God of our fathers," but also with the God of Jesus and with Jesus, who was also called "*kyrie*," "lord."

Church state traditions especially starting with Constantine constructed an imperialist and ecclesiastical idolatry. The distortion through these views indeed became excessively oppressive and should be rejected. This includes the historical as well as the contemporary misuse of the terms to justify idolatrous, governmental, or ecclesiastical oppression. This is a misuse, not only of authority, but also of the best of the biblical tradition.

Dogma is an enduring truth. For feminists this is the innate dignity of woman. Dogmatics, or the organizing of related truths, can become "dogmatic" in the pejorative sense. The more culturally conditioned or static, the more tempting is the idolatrous or absolutist position. The dogmatism of "truth" can spread even to minutiae.

Insofar as feminists assume a closed position, that there is only one way to see an issue, they succumb to a position as absolutist as that they oppose. On the other hand, their growth in feminist consciousness gives them new ways of seeing how oppressive sexism is. They need to develop clear principles and teaching which can be developed and disseminated until the oppression is massively reduced and even eliminated.

Although *Systematics* is a theological work, more and more scholars are referring to systematic injustice, systematic racism, or systematic sexism.

In most of world history as we know it, racism and sexism are so systematized, they are assumed as natural truths, or as the way things are, even the way things were "created." The horrors of this systematization are obvious in the use of a biblical rationalization of slavery in the early periods of American history or in the defense for centuries in South Africa of apartheid.

Sexism has been similarly blatant in the systematized hunting and killing of witches in colonial America and in the medieval Rhineland. Certain premises are posited and various positions follow and are developed.

Unfortunately today racism and sexism are still systematized. Fighting such systems or systematics is a world wide challenge in every culture.

An oppressive systematics exists where it is assumed in China that a male embryo or infant is innately worth more than a female embryo or infant. From such a premise follow economic, cultural, and familial judgments which result in life for the male and death for the female.

In Manila, it is assumed that male tourists have a right to buy sex with a female. In the countryside a female teenager is often an economic liability because food and money are limited. There follows the development of an economic system whereby families sell or encourage these females to "take a job" in the city. Generally the understanding of the system recognizes the deception or euphemisms which translate "job" as "prostitution." An "education" or "professional induction" takes place which is systematized, assumed as "natural," and which often develops unquestioned. Unfortunately, Manila is not unique. All over the world are parallel examples.

In the development of feminist consciousness, since the middle of the twentieth century, some women have become more and more aware of this systematized sexism. Some take action, or develop careers to address these wrongs. Some are concerned but feel helpless to address such wrongs. Others try, but are discouraged by cultural differences, differences of consciousness, or the gigantic size of the systematic oppressions.

As feminists developed their positions in the last century, they recognized the need for organizations and cross cultural dialogues. An outstanding example of this was the UN Fourth World Conference on Women which met in Beijing in 1995 when women from various backgrounds presented and discussed needs and solutions. It was in the NGO (nongovernmental organizations) forum where, despite official and unofficial hindrances, women from around the world found support and affirmation for their concerns and hopes.

Also in the twentieth century in the intellectual realm, women scholars created women's caucuses in various professional organizations. For example, the women's caucus in the American Academy of Religion addressed the need to put forth women candidates for offices. When an all male slate was proposed, the women's caucus presented the position that this was unacceptable, that the following year they would provide resumes of women with appropriate credentials, and that they expected the nominating committee to include women on the slate of candidates. Of course, women also have to be ready to be put forward, to assume positions of leadership, and to do the work involved.

Putting some women forward, however, does not necessarily change the system. In fact, it usually proves to be temporary. Although more American women now run for political office, win, and carry out their duties effectively as mayors, as representatives, as senators, they soon recognize that, if sexism is not on the surface--it usually is--it certainly is at deeper levels.

Women scholars developed understanding of women's ways of knowing, of women's ways of doing ethics, of women's medicine, but these so far have had little impact on dominant theories of knowing, on dominant ways of doing ethics, on general ways of doing medicine.

Towards the end of the last century, women scholars began to recognize the need for more systematic ways of asking the questions. A women's study group in the Catholic Biblical Association recognized the need for method. Their insight was that various members were assuming the use of certain methodological premises or processes which the individuals themselves or the others were not making explicit and which therefore were open to critique. They devised a sequence whereby they would study method in subsequent meetings.

Another group were led to ask the question of basic anthropology. Their studies led to the publication of the book *In the Embrace of God*.[15] So the pieces are being addressed and some have made progress in relating their empirical level of sensing, perceiving, imagining, feeling, speaking, moving to their intellectual level. In that level, many have learned to inquire, come to understand, express what is understood, and sort out principles and implications. On the rational level, they reflect, accumulate evidence, and judge validity. They operate on the responsible level by recognizing their goals, actions, and decisions.[16]

Nevertheless, if they are wise and sufficiently experienced, they recognize their limitations, the transcendent quality of human experience, and they walk in awe before the size and complexity, not only of human life, but also of the world and of the universe.

Ultimately, whatever the pain, whatever the joy, whatever the failures and successes, there is mystery.[17] Insofar as women individually or together achieve some measure of justice which they can call success, they are challenged by continually working out continuity, development, evaluation and revision.[18] They cannot make the mistake of presuming that one event of achieving justice can be generalized to all events, or even be characteristic of other similar events. Because some women have achieved the right to ordination in their traditions, it does not follow that all women have achieved the right to ordination in their traditions. And sadly, even though women in some traditions have been ordained, they have learned that justice and equality of opportunity still have to be fought for. Few women are called to be senior pastors, and often in a given call, a man is preferred over a woman by reason of gender.

So there is necessary on-going collection of data, interpretation, organizing, structuring, and educating. For systematic racism and sexism, there does not seem to be a ready-made justice which can easily replace such ingrained injustice. Women, however, will continue to work toward such justice. "Let justice roll down like waters" (Amos 5:24).

For Lonergan, *Communications* flow from the other Functional Specialties. This final specialty is of great importance.[19] Lonergan distinguishes four functions of meaning. 1) Meaning is cognitive, that is, real. 2) It constitutes one's horizon, powers, knowledge, values, and character. 3) It communicates to the hearer, seer, observer a possible share in the meaning of the communication. 4) If it is effective, it persuades others to action.[20]

Communications depend on and sometimes form community. A community is a group which shares a common meaning. Such meaning is usually dependent on and the result of a common field of experience. Without such commonality, persons misunderstand, distrust, and even resort to violence. This common meaning constitutes the individual as well as the community. People become who they are through their interaction with other people.

In Lonergan's view, divergent meaning may be the effect of a diversity of culture or class structures. The more serious problem comes from intellectual, moral, or religious conversion or the lack of each. These insights have important implications for feminism.

In the first place, culture provides a major division among women. In the women's movements of the 1970's and 1980's, originators of feminism in the United States assumed that all women would share their enthusiasm and insights. They didn't realize that their white middle class values would not translate to Black or Latina women in the United States, much less to women from African or Asian cultures. They expected a world wide support for their causes and were non-plused when they met, not only with lack of support, but often with opposition. They were also surprised to find that even among white middle class women there were divergences. As they recognized diversities of class structures and world views, they also found that many women from "blue collar" world views were not open to their values. In fact, they often opposed them.

Levels or types of education also affected the openness to or opposition to feminism. In some groups, women perceived by some as most in need of support of women's rights were least open to a conversion or openness of consciousness. Single mothers enthralled in poverty, young married women, or mothers dependent on a husband's income or on perceived or real power recognized implicitly that to be open to feminism was to jeopardize their economic and relational situation, even if this included alcohol, drugs, or abuse. Conversion or differentiation of consciousness is not just a matter of education, although education can be a powerful tool.

Morality implies a moral conversion or world view with implicit and/or explicit moral values, perception of what is right or not right. Much of morality is learned with the learning of language and the influence of family or family surrogates, as well as peer interaction, and sometimes modeling or mentoring.

Many of the white North American women originating and developing feminism learned moral values and concepts of justice from their families, either through identifying with them or reacting against them. Their college and sometimes high school educations were often significant adjuncts.

Particularly significant for many were the experiences of the 1960's with political involvement, organizational involvement, growth in consciousness of justice, injustice, rights and institutional critique. Various kinds of oppression were called into question. Authority, especially patriarchal or male authority, was recognized as systemic and personal oppression.

As women discovered women's ways of knowing, they created new theories of knowledge, new epistemologies. In parallel fashion, women's ways of judging or acting resulted in the development of feminist ethics.

Besides the effect of intellectual and moral conversions, or the lack of them, religious conversion or its lack significantly affected the development of feminism. Many of the advocates or originators of feminist consciousness came from the more open groups of Jewish or Christian world views. Freedom was acknowledged as a good. Liberation was not only seen as a biblical theme associated with the Exodus, but also as a spiritual and even political good associated with the New Testament. Paul's Letter to the Galatians was called the Gospel of Christian freedom. Jesus was seen as a liberator. In developing their Jewishness or Christianity, many of these women discovered a freedom which pushed them to critique patriarchal world views or structure. For some, this led to involvement in religious structures, even theological training, or ordination. For others it led to more shared responsibility and roles in marriage. For others it led to divorce. For many, development of consciousness led to rejection of Judaism or Christianity, and sometimes to secularism or goddess religions.

Some in more conservative religious traditions often left those traditions or found an accepted leadership role, sometimes gender specific. Others reinforced their conservative traditions and affirmed their traditional women's roles. Many of these conservatives were taught that "feminism" is not biblical. Insofar as the Bible, then, is interpreted as male dominant, women in these world views find their "fulfillment" in gender specific roles. For these, feminism is the work of Satan.

So intellectual, moral, and/or religious conversions are more diverse than Lonergan develops or implies. They are affected by culture, class structures, education, and other institutions. This analysis brings us to posit, in addition to these three conversions or differentiations of consciousness, a fourth, a feminist conversion or differentiation of consciousness. Each implies standing within an ideology which finds it difficult, if not impossible, to understand those whose conversion or growth in consciousness has been different.

CHAPTER IV:

FEMINISM AND CLASSICAL MODELS: GREEK, ROMAN, AND HEBREW WORLD VIEWS

Chapter Four:
Feminism and Classical Models

The first comparison we will examine is that between the classical world views represented by Greek and Roman environments, as well as the traditional Hebrew social and literary constructs.

Greek World Views

The Greek traditions we are concerned with are represented by Plato, Aristotle, Socrates, and other Greek writers. What are some of the strengths of these traditions? We can name several.

First of all, we highlight the development of reason. The word <u>reason </u>is related to <u>ratio</u>, relationship, reasonableness. Its basis is mathematical, the concept of proportion. The Greeks developed the idea of beauty based on relationship, such as the relationship of three parts to five parts. The architectural remains we can see around the Mediterranean as well as the classical models in Washington, D.C. and other cities represent this concept of relationship of parts and beauty. Connected with this is the concept of order or right relationships.

We can see the connection then with the anthropology developed by the Greeks. Beauty and diversity are related to proportion. Since it was men who were developing or who today usually represent this view, inductive reasoning points out the perfection of the parts of man related to the whole. Male genitalia and male ways of thinking are assumed to be the norm. Therefore a woman is lacking or imperfect, of even half a man.

Plato developed an anthropology of idealism, positing ideals, including souls, existing out in the universe, which are inserted into the material body and which leave the body at death.

Aristotle critiqued and improved on the model by developing a theory of form and matter which is more wholistic and which better corresponds with some modern theories of human analysis and physics. Aquinas adopted Aristotle's insights and models for developing his theology, bringing a rational perspective, but also unfortunately appropriating Aristotle's view of the perfection of man and the imperfection of woman.

The breakthrough of the Greek insights beginning with the fourth century BCE was to look at human experience in new ways and to ask the human questions in new ways. What does it mean to be human ? What is the nature of the human? How do persons reflect on human experience?

Such reflection found expression in the classic dramas of Euripides and others, as well as in the romantic poetry of Sappho. The literature also provided for the development of literary theory which Aristotle articulated and which served as structural critique in various centuries for the analysis of literature. It still serves today as one basis for literary criticism. Related is a parallel rhetorical criticism or analysis of speech acts.

An important part of Greek drama are the protest movements of women characters who defy the assumed male values, especially in the interest of peace, in defying accepted cultural norms, and in a thrust toward justice. In such dramas, we have examples of women who defy the norms as oppression, even to the cost of their lives. They know the accepted social norms, but they speak as minority voices to claim the right of proper burial for the vanquished, to articulate the injustice of loss of wealth or status. In spite of even the threat of death, they voice just values and the rights of those defeated.

Feminists today recognize the injustice of the social roles portrayed; they recognize the strength of a culture that in its major dramas, and through its greatest poets can give voice to women's cries of protest against injustice.

What can women today learn from a reading of this ancient Greek culture? They can acknowledge, sadly, that 2400 years later there are still too many in too many cultures which assume a similar world view of woman as minority and subject to men. Many today do not even allow a voice parallel to that of the Greek women. Too many poets, especially male poets, do not give political voice to women.

Women today can also learn that each culture has its assumed world views. What women in North America presume as obvious and desirable, women in Thailand may not relate to at all.

What can those who still espouse a world view comparable in its values to classical Greece learn from feminists? That whatever the customs, women have a claim to human dignity. That they can see injustice. That they can act against injustice, even at the cost of their lives. They can learn that slavery existed in ancient Greece, but that democracy also emerged there. In spite of contemporary slaveries, women can speak out, women can think, women can critique. Steps may be slow, but poets and those who act can at least name the injustices as well as the hopes.

Roman World Views

There are may similarities between the roles of women in Greek and in Roman culture. Recent research enlarges our understanding of what these roles may have been. [21] A small group of women we may call aristocratic. These women were freeborn and usually wealthy. They could inherit estates, own property, and divorce. Wealth and inheritance gave them access to public events, even public offices and building projects. Sometimes they were patrons.

A second class of women were freedwomen. Many were workers, even entrepreneurs. Some became wealthy. Among them were prostitutes or madams of brothels. Some women born free shared in many of the same class characteristics.

Slavery was prevalent in the Mediterranean world. Women slaves served in any needed activity. It was assumed that slaves were sexually available.

Roles for each level were assumed to have certain characteristics as appropriate for public or private activity. Generally, the lower the class level, the more the women might appear in public places. Occasionally aristocratic women would take part in banquets, on separate couches for women or by sitting at the foot of their husband's couch. However, they would depart after the dinner and before the "symposium" which included entertainment, drinking, discussion, and often raucous behavior.

In contrast to aristocratic women, some free women were courtesans who specialized in being available for discussion, entertainment, and sexual activity. Among free women and slaves were multiple levels, depending on their own potential power and wealth or lack of these strengths, or the power and wealth of their patrons.

Do these world views raise any questions for our contemporary worlds, and the worlds of feminism? At first sight, there may seem to be no parallels, but if we look worldwide, we are surprised at the parallels. Although slavery is illegal in most of the world, it still prevails in fact, if not technically according to law. There is the slavery of prostitution world wide in a variety of cultures. There is the slavery sometimes associated with illegal immigrants who live in fear and can claim no rights. There is the slavery of women in abusive relationships who see no way out. It is ironic that Rome at least had a structure by which slaves could buy their way to freedom.

Where these slaveries still exist, feminists can learn of the realities, and can work through law and other means to improve the situations. Feminists can realize how fragile their own freedoms are, how easily they or their friends can lose their freedom.

Those in slavery or near slavery can glimpse a dignity they might know as "feminist" that may give them hope for escape or for striving as a group to improve their situations and those of their children.

What about the sexually dominated worlds of the freedwomen of Roman society? Buying and selling, providing services, whether domestic or sexual, were the parameters of many. Is this true today? Unfortunately, yes. The sexual hassles, discriminations, requirements, and oppressions are often part of local as well as regional or world wide business today. It is little consolation to know that these things prevailed in other societies.

What can feminists learn? That whatever the freedoms they may have achieved, such freedoms are the exceptions to the status of most women.

In what ways do our worlds today resemble the sexually dominated exploitation of the Roman worlds? Unfortunately, in too many ways. Sexual services, whether to a husband, a business associate, a boss, a pimp, or a "customer" are the lot of millions of women.

The twenty-first century adds some new environments by reason of global advertising and the artificial models of feminine "beauty" which sometimes result in thousands of women being subject to eating disorders.

How can feminists recognize the systemic slavery that structures too much of our worlds? How can they claim freedom for themselves, but also recognize and develop their solidarity with sexually exploited women in their own environments as well as in world wide contexts? How is their freedom or the lack of it related to women's freedom next door, in the next apartment, the next office, or across the ocean?

The relations of wealth, power, and poverty structured the Roman worlds. Those same qualities structure our worlds. How can feminism address the needs of the increasing percentage and numbers of women in poverty, as well as their children, whether the children are with their mothers, or alone on the streets? If a feminist is independently wealthy, or has acquired a comfortable wealth, what is her relationship to a woman whose check does not provide food to last a month? How will the increasing poverty, sexual and power exploitation affect global economy and global freedom?

Hebrew World Views

In the Hebrew world views described in the Jewish scriptures, women were often sexually exploited, counted as property, counted as less than other possessions such as animals. By the first century of the common era, there were as now various traditions related to the status of women. There were and are the more conservative attitudes which see women as primarily wives and child-bearers, whose place is in the home, not in public places, and not with men.

There are those influenced by changing mores, who like many of the Jewish women of the first century loosen conservative structures and adopt other ways, whether it be the Hellenism of the first century or the secularism of the twenty-first century. It seems that many Jewish women in the first century did not need to submit to the dominance of sexuality characteristic of Hellenism or of Roman mores. On the other hand, as they led lives more in the public sphere, they were more influenced by the degradation around them. Herodias and her daughter at Herod's banquet[22] are flagrant examples of the decadence some had reached.

Many Jewish women today are searching for ways to maintain themselves in the Jewish tradition, but at the same time not submit to the required second class status. How to do that without violating the traditions is no easy task. Some are creating new rituals. Others are being ordained rabbis. Some lead scholarly groups. Some provide leadership in service groups.

Is Jewish feminism a contradiction in terms? Many think not. But other feminists can learn from them both solidarity in their efforts and awareness of their common suffering. Jewish women can learn from feminists courage in a common endeavor, critique of and reconstruction of texts, critique of and reconstruction of rituals, critique of and reconstruction of practices.

In summary, Greek, Roman, and Jewish traditions, whether lived in the first century or in their modern counterparts can learn much from feminists. They can learn to critique their world views, to acknowledge the inequalities, and to strive for greater dignity and freedom.

On the other hand, feminists can recognize the breadth both historically and culturally, especially in our root traditions, of the oppressions of women, of the indignities to which they are subjected, of the courage of some to transcend boundaries and seek freedom. They can recognize that, in some ways, some women have overcome some of these oppressions, but the successes are limited and usually culturally or economically confined. Women have only begun to claim their rightful dignity.

CHAPTER V:
FEMINISM, CHRISTIANITY, AND MAINLINE PROTESTANTISM

Chapter Five:
Feminism and Christianity

Some Christians are feminists. Some Christians who start out as feminists find that trying to de-patriarchalize Christianity is a hopeless task and therefore leave Christianity. Others realize the challenge, but decide to stay within the structures, working to bring more equality for women from within. Others reject feminism as unbiblical, even un-Christian. It is helpful to look at various traditions within Christianity to see what Christians can learn from feminists and what feminists can learn from various Christian traditions.

"Main line" Protestants

"Main line" Protestants are diverse. In general, the term refers to members in those churches extending more directly from the Protestant Reformation, and from the leadership of Luther or Calvin. Although their membership in the United States has sometimes been seen as declining in the last decades, they still embody a principal set of traditions which were at the founding of many structures in the United States. These still influence our leadership, both nationally and locally. They have been formative for many of our national and local leaders.

Some terms are applied, appropriately or not, to aspects of these traditions. Some Protestants are in the liberal tradition. They believe Christianity must accommodate itself to a scientific world view and to insights from the modern sciences. Christianity must be able to correlate with experience and reason. This affects interpretation of the Bible as well as beliefs and ethics. Authority, including biblical authority, interacts with experience and reason. Reason and revelation are not opposites, but complementary. Liberals embrace human potential movements. From this also follow social justice activities to bring God and human beings together.

It is relatively easy to see how many could grow in their espousal of feminism out of a liberal Protestant tradition. The emphases on freedom, human potential, social justice provide foundations for women to claim full dignity. In that way, most liberal Protestant traditions gradually developed readiness for the approval of women's ordination. On the other hand, women's ordination has not solved the problem of discrimination against women. The call or appointment to be senior pastor is still dominantly given to a man over a woman.

What can feminists and liberal Protestants learn from each other? That basic changes in human relationships are not easily won. That changes in legal or juridical structures usually require much work and leadership. That individual and social identities are woven into world views and they are not easily modified. That, on the other hand, it is possible to make strides in respect for human dignity, that laws can be changed, that only gradually do we see and deal with effects of juridical change, that supporters are not necessarily to be counted on, but may come from unexpected quarters.

A second set of traditions is associated with "main line" Protestant conservatism. For conservatives, God is the author of the Bible. God inspired the Biblical Word which is foremost and foundational. Although the doctrine of the Trinity is basic, dominance is given to Christ. Christ was born of a virgin, atoned for sins, was bodily resurrected, and will come again.

Starting in the 1930's was the growth of neo-orthodoxy, new or renewed foundational teachings. The Christian revelation is unique. Christ alone is the revelation. The resurrection of Christ is a mighty act of God and the means of human salvation. Human beings are sinners, but may be justified and given new life in Christ.

For the most part, conservative Protestantism is not open to feminism. Authoritative and traditional structures honor the dignity of women, but see woman's place in more traditional roles. Feminists can learn about the strength and importance of authority and tradition in culture and in the spiritual life.. They can acknowledge the resistance of many women who find contentment in their roles and in their structures. There is a certainty and a safety which work well for many women. They can grow and accomplish much without being a threat to structures.

On the other hand, conservatives can learn that many women find such roles limiting and confining. If they can't make changes and find growth in their conservative milieu, they feel forced to leave those traditions. Sometimes they search for and find others. Sometimes they just abandon these traditions--with or without guilt.

Evangelical Theology

Evangelical Theology is a broad based term that can signify different images to different persons. In one way, all Christianity is evangelical. The word comes from the New Testament and denotes spreading the good news of Jesus. In the last century a group with the English writer C.S. Lewis founded the National Association of Evangelicals in 1942. They opposed extremes of literalism associated with the name fundamentalism but also rejected what they saw as a liberal Protestant ecumenical movement which they thought had lost the centrality of Jesus and biblical foundations.

Most, if not all, evangelicals affirm verbal inerrancy and the primacy of the Bible with an avoidance or rejection of historical-critical method and so called higher criticism. By the

1960's, however, some evangelicals recognized the importance of using a critical historical-theological method. The ethical teachings of the Bible are interpreted in a tradition related to received Biblical teachings. The personal dimension of relationship with Jesus, and fellowship in community, are seen as constituting the church. Some evangelicals are referred to as the "New Evangelicals." Here there is more interest in the social dimension of Christianity, in whole persons, even in dialogue with other Christian groups. There is a rediscovery of Karl Barth and that part of the Reform tradition following from his work. In some urban areas, the enthusiasm, commitment, and welcoming have attracted large numbers, especially of young working adults, and young families. They find belief and support systems for personal commitment, children, family life, and outreach. In some cases, they build schools and other formalized structures to meet educational and social needs, whether of the young, the middle, or the older members. Those who join find a welcoming community.

What can feminists learn from evangelicals, and what can evangelicals learn from feminists? Virginia Ramey Mollenkott is an evangelical theologian who addresses these issues. In such books as *The Divine Feminine: Biblical Imagery of God as Female* and *Godding: Human Responsibility and the Bible,* she acknowledges that

> To be one with God means to recognize our oneness with all those who have also derived their being from the same source: Muslims; Jews; post-Christian or post-Jewish feminists; gay people or heterosexual people; liberal or fundamentalist people; communist or capitalist people; black, white, red, or yellow people.[23]

While many if not most evangelicals would be uncomfortable with this language, at the same time it reflects a new reaching out while maintaining a strong Christocentric commitment that characterizes some of the growing evangelical churches.

From evangelicals, feminists can learn the importance of religious commitment, the importance of community, the current need for diverse activities for diverse groups, the importance of celebrating with music and sometimes other arts. Evangelicals can learn that some women are seeking positions of leadership appropriate to their call, their abilities, and their education. They can strive to be open to new questions and to changes which can be as challenging as those faced by Paul's communities in Corinth and in Rome in the first century of the apostolic church.

Catholicism, Roman and Otherwise

"Christian" names all those who follow Christ. In distinction from the reformers following Luther, Calvin, and others, medieval Christianity modulated through the Council of Trent in the sixteenth century, and centering in Rome, becomes "Roman Catholicism." Although Anglicanism and some other traditions retain the Catholic nomenclature, we will look first at the varieties of traditions stemming from Roman Catholicism. Geographically and institutionally, Roman Catholicism continues from the first century centering in Peter in Rome and the continuity of bishops there in spite of the Constantinian reforms centering in Constantinople.

Necessarily assuming a defensive position at Trent, Roman Catholicism cleaned up many of the scandals of the middle ages, organized its seminaries, and structured its clergy by indoctrination as well as by obedience. Colonialism created its various nationalistic varieties of Catholicism in Central and Latin America, in Asia, India, and Africa. Besides the layers of colonialism, large immigrations, especially of Irish, German, Polish, and Italian Catholics created strong Catholic communities in the United States and in other parts of the world in the nineteenth and twentieth centuries. The diverse experiences of World War II, followed by mobile growth of corporations and jobs, raised questions for those who had lived in enclave mentalities. Fragmentation continued in the 1960's with the influx of secularism, anti-war and civil rights movements. At the same time, Pope John XXIII at the Vatican Council II opened the windows to new ideas, recovery of biblical roots, inter-faith dialogues, and more democratic discussions.

As a result, there are many kinds of Catholics in the twenty-first century. There are reactionaries who reject newness and are reclaiming or reaffirming a Catholicism close to pre-Vatican II world views. At the opposite end are those who have given up, joined Protestant churches, or abandoned hope of finding a church community with which they share values. In between are various individuals or groups who continue their commitments within Catholicism in various strains of conservatism, moderation, or liberalism.

At the conservative end are those women who like things the way they are, who continue to live in and support or ignore Catholic patriarchal structures. At the other end are those women who felt they could not respect such patriarchal structures. Some left religion altogether or opted for goddess, pagan, or nature religions. Others took courage from the feminist movements as well as from their recovery of scripture and worked within the structures to open them more for women. Some of these call themselves feminists. Some do not. Some maintain their Christianity and their Catholicism within feminist world views, which are often ignored or disapproved of by official Catholic authorities.

What can feminists learn from Roman Catholicism? What can Roman Catholics learn from feminists? Roman Catholicism has survived for almost 2000 years. In the New Testament, its primary scripture, it proclaims:

In Christ there is not

Jew or Gentile,

slave or free,

male and female (Gal 3:28).

It proclaims a new freedom in Christ. It holds up a Jesus who respected women and men and called them forth to new life. For many women these texts and stories provide a constitution for working for freedom and for the coming of the kingdom. There are world wide networks to support and communicate this freedom. The structures and the networks are so worldwide that certain kinds of local integrity can grow and continue without condemnation from authorities.

Not only the scriptures, but the systems of symbols embodied in liturgy and theology can be interpreted to call women to freedom. Baptism provides a universality, a depth of dying and rising which empowers many women to claim their call and their ministry. Eucharist is giving of thanks and communion in which all are one in Christ. Yes, these symbols also have patriarchal accouterments which contradict the basic symbols. Some women ignore these. Some work to redeem them and free them from patriarchy. Feminists can learn the complexity of symbols and structures, can learn that empowering symbols come in many forms and cultures, that truth can even ride on false or contradictory symbols.

What can Roman Catholicism learn from feminists? That inflexibility of structures and refusal to acknowledge how structures oppress women can lead to loss of women and men leaders of all kinds. It can learn that oppression can be carried in structures for thousands of years. It can acknowledge its responsibility in women's oppression for thousands of years. It can learn courage to make necessary changes. It can learn to trust the spirit for what God may be calling for in the twenty-first century.

Other traditions which retain the Catholic tradition have often split on what may be considered women's issues. Some Anglican and Episcopal traditions now ordain women. They find no scriptural or traditional prohibitions against ordination. Others have retained the male-only doctrine. Some of the latter have even converted as a group to Roman Catholicism. Feminists can learn how divisive some of their tenets may be.

But they can also learn that change can take place, even against very strong odds.

Liberation Theology

"Liberation Theology" became a world wide phrase with the publication in 1971 of *A Theology of Liberation: History, Politics and Salvation* by Gustavo Gutierrez of Lima, Peru.[24] Such theology calls for the liberation of the oppressed. It calls for changing the political, economic, and social forces which are the systems of oppression.

In the 1960's, a ferment for change developed in Latin America which focused on the dehumanized situations of most of the poor. Some leaders called for a Marxist critique of economic structures and for a recognition of the rights of the poor. In Latin America three groups traditionally dominate: the land owners, the military, and the church. Often the three are intertwined. Critiques led to political movements and to revolution. Thus Cuba became an anti-church communist state. Central America and the Caribbean became embroiled in civil wars, class wars, and continuing corporate colonization, especially from North

America. For the most part, South America succumbed to dictators and/or multi-national corporate economic dominance.

In religious experience, base or faith communities grew which helped some poor persons develop literacy, leadership, and political critiques. A Catholic bishop in Brazil, Dom Helder Camara, became a voice for the poor. Several Catholic priests, such as Camilo Torres and Che Guevara, sided with the poor, left their clerical positions, provided leadership for social revolutionaries, and were eventually assassinated or killed in war.

In 1966 at a meeting of the World Council of Churches, Gonsalo Cardenas said that "Revolution can be peaceful if the minorities [the rich and powerful] do not resist violently..."[25] Richard Shaull advocated small groups willing to engage in subversive acts.[26] At a conference of Latin American Roman Catholic bishops, documents expressed concern for the poor and indicated that people must be liberated in personal, social, and national contexts, whatever the sacrifice. An example of a peasant woman who emerged from this context is Rigaberto Menchu, winner of the 1992 Nobel peace prize.

Liberation theology became more global and at the same time, more divided as it became more international. In 1976 at a meeting in Africa, theologians recognized how culturally diverse are Third World theologians. While poverty and oppression are universal challenges, racial and class discrimination, as well as the minority status of Christians in many countries, add dimensions culturally different from those of Latin Americans.[27]

What can feminists learn from liberation theology and what can liberation theology learn from feminism? The answers are developing in the interaction of Third World theologians from Africa, Asia, and Latin America. Africa is as diverse as the indigenous and colonial peoples of which it is constituted. Asia requires acknowledgment of Hindu, Buddhist, Islamic, communist, or secular domination and the contrast between the world views of Christianity and the world views of the dominant religions or cultures. Latin America is beginning to recognize the diversity of the indigenous cultures as well the mixtures of bloods and cultures.

Feminism can learn how diverse are these thousands of cultures. Dignity for women in one culture may not be perceived as dignity in another culture. Certainly what some North American feminists describe as goals for feminism may not be goals agreed on by women from some other cultures. The perceived dignity of women is so intertwined with accepted roles, with economic levels, with perceived or real power, with high or low risks for sanctions, or even assassinations that generalizations are seldom simple.

On the other hand, individual women face to face often reach across cultures to identify with, or at least respect, other women. Groups of women from diverse backgrounds, working with each other at a common task often experience a bonding which transcends their particularities of culture. What is called for, then, is increasing understanding of the complexities and specificities of world views and culture. Increasing understanding must be accompanied by growth in respect for diversity, patience in transforming societies, and always growth in real dignity for women.

Theology of Suffering

A Theology of Suffering has its roots in the Gospel image of Jesus who suffered, died, and was raised up. If Christians ignore the question of suffering, they ignore as well the Jesus whose sufferings are described acutely and paradoxically by all four Gospel writers. Moreover, Paul's letters display a dominant theme of Jesus who through his suffering and death brings into being the new creation. This is not a theme which most North American feminists find congenial. On the contrary, the suffering-death image has often been misused for almost 2000 years as an instrument of oppression. Too many women have been exploited and have wrongfully accepted the role of victim, whether in marriage, or in economic or political life under the aegis of Jesus who suffered even unto death. This is perhaps one of the most insidious distortions of spirituality associated with Christianity.

Most North American feminists see suffering as a result of patriarchal structures and actions which deny women dignity, respect, and social justice. This is certainly correct in the context of women slaves, of many women prostitutes, of discrimination in the economic, political, and religious spheres. Overcoming patriarchy can open possibilities of freedom, new life, and the elimination of much suffering But overcoming patriarchy is not just equality of rights and opportunities, important as this may be.

In *The Strength of the Weak: Toward a Christian Feminist Identity,* Dorothee Soelle writes:

> ...I understand under feminism that segment of the women's movement which fights not only for the equality of women but also for a different culture...the point is not to become a vice-president of General Motors. The point is to change General Motors so radically that neither it nor we will need any more presidents or vice-presidents.[28]

This may be labeled naive, but it indicates how radical the reorientation must be. It is possible to bring about radical change through peaceful measures, but it takes an openness and mastery not frequently available. It probably cannot be brought about without some kind of suffering.

The experience of women in the Third World, however, brings a different perspective. Some with First World experience or the equivalent education may identify with North American feminists. Others may be at quite a different place where patriarchal as well as political and economic oppression is so overwhelming that they concentrate on basic human rights. Although some are still indoctrinated with suffering and victimization as a religious way of life, others find in the Exodus saga or in the freedom proclaimed by Jesus a rallying cry which gives them hope and courage to fight.

Although a theology of suffering, rightly or wrongly interpreted or abused, is integral to Christianity, some persons in the post-World War generation in Germany were especially articulate in striving to deal with the aftermath of the Holocaust. As a woman who had to wrestle with the generation who either supported Nazism or who closed their eyes to ignore it, Dorothy Soelle became a voice on radio and in her writings for naming the horror of suffering. Like others in the 1960's and in decades following, Soelle was then caught up in the protest movements against the nuclear arms build up, continuing militarization, the

Vietnam War, and the growing violation of human rights. One of her powerful books is titled *Of War and Love.*

Another German theologian Jurgen Moltmann also wrestled with the post-Holocaust questions. Paradoxically, precisely as a German prisoner of war, he experienced God. His search for hope eventuated in his major book *Theology of Hope.* But the questions raised, as well as the continuing sufferings world wide, kept him writing with even more intensity addressing global issues. A significant study is *The Crucified God.* Later titles include *Experience of God* and *The Power of the Powerless: The Word of Liberation for Today.*[29]

Especially in the later chapters of *The Crucified God,* Moltmann develops a profound theology of suffering in the context of a Theology of the Cross. He critiques an inadequate philosophical view of God as creator without reference to the Jesus on the cross. He places all of creation in the world view of the centrality of Jesus' death-resurrection . From this focus, he develops a Trinitarian theology of the cross. Such an articulation of Trinitarian theology flows from the concept of the crucified. Similarly, there is no dualism in his description of Jesus as man and Jesus as God. Moltmann follows Abraham Heschel in his articulation of the *pathos* of God.[30]

From the theology described above, Moltmann critiques a political hermeneutics of liberation and a political theology of the cross and articulates hope from the transformations of God in the liberations of human beings.[31]

What can a theology of suffering offer feminism and what can feminism offer in return? Women rightly reject unnecessary suffering and work to alleviate as much suffering as possible. Nevertheless, they know that suffering is part of the human experience. Rightly interpreted, a theology of suffering can give them a language, a set of images and symbols, a complexity of levels which name their sufferings and the sufferings of the world. God suffers with them. There can even be a redemptive aspect to their suffering. They die in Christ. But they also live in Christ. Dying is continuous, but so is the rising. Dying-Rising is a way of transforming themselves and transforming the world.

What can a theology of suffering learn from feminists? That women's experience of suffering is paradigmatic. From giving birth to the dying of others, women's bodies, hearts, and minds are one with suffering. Their experience gives them a depth of understanding which courageously rejects unnecessary suffering, which fights against even what may seem to be unavoidable suffering. Their thrust is toward Life, and it is continuing Life and resurrection which can transform suffering and death into Life. Witnesses of crucifixion, they are also able to be witnesses of resurrection.

Theology of Hope

It is surprising that Moltmann wrote *Theology of Hope* years before he wrote *The Crucified God.* In a way the first led to the second. If there is no suffering, loss, or lack, there is no need for hope. Hope comes from a broken experience.

Moltmann's exhaustive *Theology of Hope* raises many questions. Most of us think of hope in short terms. I hope she will get well. I hope we can solve this problem. I hope it will be sunny tomorrow.

Moltmann raises questions not only about long term hopes such as hope for a peaceful world, but whether there is a possibility of a totally new world. These questions are currently raised by some books and films in the science fiction genre which depict possible worlds of "Contact" and of utopian societies. More often, however, the science fiction creators depict universes of good and evil, often ones in which horrendous evils dominate. There are many who see the possibility of the triumph of good as very slight, even in the long time aeons of continuing universes.

Some millenarists, on the other hand, see the triumph of good over evil as coming soon, or not so soon, as the sudden coming of the kingdom through the action of God. This will be a kingdom of peace with no suffering.

Although Moltmann uses similar theological language, his questions are very different. He reviews questions of what we mean by history, how we project the *eschaton*, or the end of history, or the possible end of the universe, and whether God is part of human history, as the Hebrew and Christian scriptures indicate.

Out of his Lutheran tradition, Moltmann places all history, including the unfolding of the cosmos, against the death-resurrection of Christ. From this tradition he develops a cosmic view that resurrection or new creation only comes as integral with the crucifixion and death of the cosmic Christ. Even if one is uncomfortable with or rejects Moltmann's Christian language, the questions remain: can we hope for an eventual universe that doesn't include suffering, or is suffering-transformed-into-life the only possibility, and, in fact, the preferred possibility?

What can a theology of hope learn from feminists? That suffering and hope are in the concrete, in the particular. Women are suffering now. Their children are hungry now. Much as they work for improved conditions for themselves and others now, they are always aware of the hundreds of women contemporaneously being raped, battered, or killed. To some degree, utopias are an unreal luxury. Much as they may dream of and work for a universe of peace, they are bombarded on all sides by suffering, hunger, and crucifixions of all kinds.

What can feminists learn from a theology of hope? That the questions are long term. While they work for short term gains, they are part of a longer process that may bring greater hope for others as well as for themselves. Whether or not the

Christ language is congenial to them, they can relate to the integrity of death-new life. Somehow in their sufferings they are in a process of being transformed. With whatever images, they can hope for new life that gives meaning to their sufferings. They can make their cosmic contribution to whatever unfolding of human or women's history is taking place. They can see their lives as meaningful in an evolving universe. They may find helpful the image of a crucified Christ who was raised up. Their sufferings may be related to life and new creation.

CHAPTER VI:
FEMINISM AND SELECTED NON-CHRISTIAN WORLD VIEWS

Chapter Six:

Feminism and Selected
Non-Christian World Views

Three non-Christian world views will be used for the dialectic: Islam, Buddhism, and New Age. These are chosen because of their growing popularity and populations and because of the variety of backgrounds and focal points they supply. What can each learn from feminism and what can feminism learn from each of these?

Islam

For most Western feminists, Islam probably seems to be a contradiction of feminism. In some ways, this may be true. However, it is well to ask what are the complexities of Islam? What are the varieties from more fundamentalist views to perhaps more liberal views? Is there a difference between theory and practice? How significant are national differences?

One cannot explore the fullness of Islam here, but one can draw on reliable sources to at least address the questions seriously. *Islam Today, A Short Introduction to the Muslim World*, by Akbar S. Ahmed[32] will be a chief source for the dialectic.

What are the complexities of Islam? This is perhaps the hardest part to understand. Few persons in Western cultures have occasion to study Islam. If they avert to Islam at all, it is often as reaction to a news media depiction of terrorism or violence. Pictures of women tend to be those with the covering *chador.* The news also reports on women punished or arrested for being out of the home or for riding a bicycle.

The author of the book *Islam Today*, Akbar S. Akmed is a fellow of Selwyn College, Cambridge University, and has been a visiting Professor at the Institute of Advanced Study, Princeton, and at Harvard University. Ahmed acknowledges that in the West, Islam is perceived as a religion focused on converting others to its way of thinking and to an acknowledgement of Allah and the Muslim way of life.[33] Words, images, or concepts from the West are often applied perhaps inappropriately to Islam. For example, Muslims may be said to be fundamentalists in the sense that they believe in the fundamentals of their religion, the Quran and the Prophet.[34] However, to assume that such believers are fanatics or extremists does not necessarily follow.

Varieties of Islam can be looked at in the context of particular national developments. The rise of modern Turkey is an example of an Islamic state in which, although many of the leaders are Muslims, the government structures are largely non-Islamic. Nevertheless, tensions exist. Will Turkey continue to make connections with the West, or will it draw closer to other Islamic worlds?

In contrast, under the Ayatollah Khomeine, Iran spurred a revolution which identified the revival and dominance of Islam with the continuing success of the revolution. Sanctions from the West only seem to reinforce the strength of the Islamic world view against the world view represented by the USA and its allies.

India, Pakistan, and Bangladesh represent a complexity of other developments. The problem of Muslim identity faces many challenges. Pakistan has the power of the nuclear bomb, but it also has a population of women who are mostly illiterate. Large groups of Muslims in Northern Africa, Indonesia, Europe, and North America pose other varieties of more conservative or less conservative Islamic world views.

As central to Islam, the family reflects the perceived order and balance in the universe.[35] Within an extended family of three or four generations, each person has a place. Theoretically, men and women are equal. For example, women have a right to divorce. However, a man is given a larger part of an inheritance on the presumption that he must maintain wife and family.

What can Islam learn from feminism? Before one tries to answer that, one can recognize what a presumption this question is. Such a question assumes that Islamic women want to learn from Western movements, including those associated with feminism. There are some Islamic women, principally from those richer families who may interact with the West, who may wish to have some of the freedoms or rights they see in women from Western societies. On the whole, however, Islamic women are so imbued with their traditional place in the universe, that they not only do not want what they see in Western women, but, on the contrary, they abhor the blatant sexuality and exploitation which is expressed world wide through Western media. On the other hand, some Islamic women earn advanced degrees, teach at universities including those in North America, are well educated, and serve as elected representatives in parliaments or congresses.

Feminists may respond by pointing out the need for openness, that not all women can be expected to understand, respect, or even tolerate the assumed place of women in Islamic society.

Whatever the positive reasons for woman's place in Islam, the continuance, however small, of polygamy, the continuance of the custom of arranged marriages, the separation of women and men for meals, customs of seclusion, the *chador* or veiling, are for the most part seen by Western women, including feminists, as oppressive and divisive. Much more communication and respect are necessary for any bridging to take place. If women from diverse world views can talk with each other with respect, rather than defense, perhaps families and even societies can learn to live at least side by side with mutual tolerance.

Buddhism

Buddhism has a tradition, extending from six hundred years before the common era until now, which theoretically emphasizes the equality of men and women. After leaving a life of luxury to find a way of freeing persons from suffering, Gautama Buddha became a wandering ascetic to seek enlightenment and to teach a way of freedom from suffering, sickness, old age, and despair.

It is understandable how women now and through the centuries relate to the Four Noble Truths: 1) the relationship of life and suffering; 2) the recognition that suffering is caused by our desires; 3) acknowledgement of a state in which there is no suffering; and 4) that such a state can be achieved. Women can agree that the way to eliminate suffering is through the eightfold path of right understanding, right thought, right speech, right action, right livelihood, right effort, right mindfulness, and right meditation.

Acceptance of inevitable change and flux leads to detachment. Meditation can quiet the mind and bring about enlightenment. Possible is an ultimate enlightened state of *nirvana*.

Historically, for example, this movement has allowed for the development of monasteries of women in Tibet and also in exile in India or elsewhere with their own traditions and structures. However, it was and still is acknowledged that the first place Buddhist nun will still be after the lowest male Buddhist monk.

From the middle of the twentieth century, Buddhism has grown world wide. North Americans and Europeans traveled to India and Tibet and brought back Buddhism to their countries. With the political ferment of India, Tibet, China, and South Asia, teachers, monks, and nuns often fled from Asia and settled in North America or France. Southern France, as well as certain cities in North America, became centers and attracted converts from many places. As educated women became part of these developments, some women have become teachers and nuns.

Master Hsing Yun of Taiwan presided over the full ordination of 135 nuns in 1998.[36]

Besides continuing to practice compassion, some Buddhists are facing the needs of modern times and are engaging in social activism. Thich Nhat Hanh has become a leader in peace writings and peace action. More recently the Dalai Lama has also been reaching out to address peace themes explicitly. For some, this leads to marching for peace, working against land mines, and working for environmental causes. In the villages of Sri Lanka a movement called *Sarvodaya* has involved thousands of monks working with villagers for community improvement.

What does all this mean for feminism? In Tibet-in-exile camps in India, with the support of North American women, Buddhist nuns are improving their education and striving to stabilize their traditions. A significant number of North American or European women have become teachers in Buddhist meditation. Some women have shaved their heads and donned Buddhist robes as nuns and others have become ordained teachers.

Feminists can learn that some women are hungry for a tradition of compassion and meditation. Some are finding that tradition in Buddhism. The theory if not the practice of equality of women and men encourages those women who continue in Buddhism.

Buddhist women can learn from feminists that whatever the theory, the inequality of opportunity in practice for women militates against the full potential of freedom. Buddhist women may find freedom from suffering through their meditation and practices, but full equality seems to be far in the future.

New Age

What does "New Age" connote? It depends on the participants in the discussion. If the discussant is within a fundamentalist or more conservative tradition, the person probably reacts negatively, and provides a polemic. Practitioners of "New Age" may even be seen as doing the work of Satan.

A different response may come from those familiar with the "Age of Aquarius," as popularized in the 1960's. Images incorporate a new age of peace and prosperity in which all will love one another, there will be harmony with the earth and on the earth, and common people will transcend cultural and political differences. A new wisdom of consciousness makes full communication possible.

Somewhat surprisingly in this context, the "life of the ages" and the image of a "new covenant" or way of being, belong to the Jewish and Christian traditions as a way of imaging the ideal and looking forward to a time of righteousness.

It is no wonder, then, that "New Age" involves an eclecticism which suggests a wide variety of ideas as divergent as Plato's idealism, Swedenborgianism, and astrology. Whatever its parameters, "New Age" images appeal to many persons today, especially those hungry for a sensory wholistic vision of the present and future emphasizing the fullness of human consciousness and a hope for unity.

People who relate to "New Age" are often educated in psychology or the social sciences, but find a lack which draws them to a philosophic or mystical bent. They find nourishment in some aspects of "Eastern" thought, in physiological/

neurological characteristics of consciousness, in a somewhat mystical relationship with the earth and the universe, and in a perception of the oneness of the universe. They often develop an awareness of the possibility of communication through extra-sensory perception. They posit the existence of intelligent beings in the universe other than human, some communicating across time and place. They feel connected to these possibilities of communication. An existence that continues into an indefinite or infinite future transcends the limitations perceived by most persons.

It is easy to see then why fundamentalist or more conservative traditions cannot tolerate "New Age." "New Age" is understood as too eclectic, as anti-dogmatic, as anti-Christ, or as anti-Allah, in fact, diabolic.

On the other hand, what is its appeal to the millions of persons who buy the books, publish the books, create the music, buy the CD's, and practice various rituals, exercises, or thought processes which are within the movement? Why do so many from the mainline religious traditions add aspects of "New Age" to their own traditions, or move gradually from their traditions to world views more characterized as "New Age"? Why are there so many current or former Protestants or Catholics who find more fulfillment in "New Age" thought processes, rituals, or music than they do in their more traditional world views?

Against this background, what can feminists learn from "New Age" and what can "New Age" learn from feminists? Feminists can learn that many persons, especially women, are hungry for spiritual and mystical support, experiences, and education. They want to be freed to the universe. They want to see the relationship between their inner life and the life of the universe. They want a relationship with a significant other that is deep and not superficial. This transcends many of the goals and horizons of various feminisms.

What can "New Age" learn from feminism? That "New Age" can often be an avoidance of the basic needs of feminism. It can be an escape from the injustices which pervade most world views prevalent in society. Some women may escape from the inferiority of a dominantly patriarchal society. However, even here, the gurus are often male. And what about the majority of women in the world who are exploited economically, sexually, politically, religiously? Where or when is the "New Age" for them?

CHAPTER VII:
BEYOND FEMINISM

Chapter Seven:

Beyond Feminism: Model for
A Theological Reflection for the Next Aeon

What are some ways we can provide a model for theological reflection in the 21st century which includes insights from feminism and other world views which have similar concerns for women?

One model is a process of five steps which interact with each other in a non-linear way to frame the human concern for meaning. The five steps are: 1) experience; 2) expression; 3) reflection; 4) commitment; 5) proclamation. In this section, against the context of the previous chapters, we will explore the potential for developing each of these in the 21st century. They can be pointers to enlarge the insights and actions of feminism and similar world views to continually expanding horizons.

Experience

What are and will be the experience of women in the 21st century? The range is very wide. Several American women have been or are astronauts. One successfully led a shuttle mission. Several others are models for women scientists. At the other extreme are women on all continents who do not have enough food for their children.

What is theological reflection? It is an effort to understand, and therefore a process of reflective knowledge. It is the continuing interpreting of symbols so that a new world opens up. One black American woman, for example, was a child in poverty. But her family's love and her teachers' encouragement enabled her to pursue education, one level at a time, until she acquired a doctorate, was accepted into the NASA program, and became successful in a challenging and difficult field. What are the experiences and conversion points which enabled her to affirm her own abilities, to develop faith in herself and others?

Do some of these same women perhaps develop themselves and their faith in marriage and other relationships? Yes. The woman astronaut who successfully led the mission was most anxious to return to her three year old daughter. When the first woman teacher qualified for a shuttle flight and was killed, not only her family, including her children, mourned but most of America mourned with them.

What are the theological dimensions of these experiences? Most register a respect for the integrity of the human being. Many affirm a new faith in the beauty of the world seen from such a distance. In some cases, this provides an experience of a God of the universe beyond any imagining or naming. Couple that experience with returning to a three year old daughter and the miracle of life and of love and you have experiences of multiple symbols which defy the adequacy of words.

In contrast is the experience of many African women today. One woman might be a Christian in the Sudan who fears for her own life and that of her children each day because of political and religious violence. Another woman might be an indigenous woman of Central Africa who leads her community in clean water development through the digging of wells. In South Africa we have many black women who are courageously leading their children into a new world where black and white persons can respect each other, work together, and strive to overcome violence. Another woman in South Africa might be a teacher or a politician facilitating reconciliation and helping people to build structures of growth.

So the experiences of women are exceedingly diverse. For each woman, the experiences are foundational to a belief system. A woman successful in NASA might espouse traditional religious values for herself and her family. Another may find the religious values of her upbringing are inadequate to her present global perspectives. She may find she rejects those former values. She may be searching for new horizons, new images, and a new way to think about beliefs.

A Christian woman in the Sudan may be unable to experience much other than severe anxiety about survival for herself and her children. But who can guess what depth of faith and hope for the future may keep that woman going day after day?

A woman in South Africa may be white, trying to help herself and her children deal with a new society that is black and white. She may be working to cope with the increasing violence in her urban setting. She may be working with the reconciliation groups supported by Bishop Tutu to bridge the horrors of the apartheid experience. Perhaps she has been Anglican for generations. Perhaps she is a new convert. Perhaps she is living an intense mystical life, with the experience of God dominating her consciousness.

For each of these women, her experience is basic to any thoughts or questions about God. Each knows herself as woman. Some may accept the patriarchal world. Some may know the word feminism. Many will not. All hope out of their experience for more well being for themselves, their children, and society. Any theology of the future needs to be as local as their experience and as global as the diverse needs of the planet. Such theology and theological reflection start to look in many ways quite different from our traditional theologies.

Expression

Typically a person brings the experience to expression. What form does the expression take? The possibilities are seemingly endless. The expression may be words which attempt to describe the experience or express emotions which relate to the experience. Rather than words, some may use artistic expression, whether dance, painting, song, or graphics. Psychological expression may take the form of sadness or joy, mourning or exuberance.

How does this work out with women in local situations? How does this relate to feminism?

We may think of a woman who runs a sheep-herding ranch in Australia. We can research or imagine a multitude of her experiences. How does she express those experiences? She may be ecstatic at the sunrises and sunsets she sees each day. She may express her experience of God in traditional Christian religious terms, in a dialogue with the being she perceives as creator related to the dynamic of nature and the sun, or simply as awe. On the other hand, her expression may be groans from a weariness of daily tasks.

Quite different may be the experience and expression of an Inuit woman at the Arctic Circle who inherits world views of symbols, myths, narratives, and actions which she has learned from her family and clan. She may articulate her daily experience in sharing with her children, family, and community the stories, rituals, symbolic thinking and acting appropriate to her culture. She may prepare foods, she may nurture her children, she may carry out actions interrelating to the gods, spirits, relationships with others, with the earth, and with the universe. She will tell her stories, sing her songs, and dance her dances as expressions of her continuing experiences.

A woman in Austria may live in an apartment with her husband. Her experiences have included wars, violence, major political and economic upsets. She may embody five generations of Roman Catholic traditions. As a caring adult, she may be active in helping to move her church into new ways of relating to the modern and future world. Her experience as an educated Catholic adult moves her to want to take responsibility for many aspects of her adult church. Her expressions may take the form of prayer, of political organizing, and of community development to speak out as a contemporary Roman Catholic woman.

Reflection

Just as experience moves to expression, so experience/ expression moves to reflection. What is reflection? *Flect* refers to bending and *re* is back, so *reflection* is bending back in thought on the experience and expression. The reflection may be deliberate as a means of growth, or it may be forced because of a negative effect on the body, or a violent change in circumstances. The reflection may take the form of a dialogue with oneself, a dialogue with another, or others. Or it may be a dialectic using the power of intellect and reason. In this way, a person or a group can lay out possible interpretations and thereby seek truth and wisdom.

Among indigenous as well as other peoples, there are many routes to reflection. A person may walk out into nature to find peace, patterns, and answers. By seeing the cycles in nature, the continuance of life-death-new life, one may see one's experience/expression in a parallel context. By seeing aspects of life, a person may gain insight to a particular experience. For example, a person may observe a bird building a nest, feeding its young, or defending its territory. There is an insight related to processes of parents, young, and growth. A caterpillar may develop its crysallis. Patient observing for about ten days can see subtle and then dramatic changes, and finally the emergence of a monarch butterfly. Gazing at the Northern Lights, the movement of the planets, the apparent infinity of the universe of stars and galaxies provide a perspective which places human experience/expression in a perspective which reaches beyond ordinary human challenges and problems.

Many North American Indians are able to reflect through their stories, myths, and rituals on their oneness with the earth, on the pervasiveness of the holy, on the importance of their traditions and way of life. With the help of a shaman, the elders, the community, a vision quest, they can reflect on their place in the universe and on the meaning of their life. It is no wonder that many non-Indians who find their lives meaningless try to adopt Indian ways to make sense of their own lives.

Dreams are a phenomenon of human experience in that humans can reflect on and interpret their dreams. Dogs and other animals dream, but as far as we can tell, they don't reflect on the meaning. Indigenous people generally value their dreams highly as resource for finding meaning, relating to the universe, and deciding on action.

With some exceptions, Western society devalues dreams as so unscientific that persons learn at an early age to repress their dreams, laugh them off, or ignore them. The great exception in modern Western development, of course, was Freud, who developed a system of interpreting dreams which led him to his theory of the power of the unconscious. In spite of his basic insights, many modern persons who espouse to be scientific, reject the absoluteness of the Freudian systems. Nevertheless, there are recurring counselors or spiritual writers who find favor by helping persons come to fuller self-understanding by interpreting their dreams.

One value of dream interpretations is the acknowledgement of the interaction of conscious and unconscious worlds, of the integrity of body-mind-soul-emotion processes. Our dreams present images of deep feelings or thought which we ordinarily ignore or even reject. To remember a dream--a night dream or a day dream--and to walk through its possible meanings is to acknowledge the body-mind-soul-emotion process. The power is not in the Freudian sense necessarily to determine cause-effect processes, but to articulate naming and relationships which create new insights for living. Some find the Jungian structures creative in providing universal symbols of light/darkness, doors/ walls or other archetypical images. Still, the value is what happens in the individual's interpretations and insights to her own situation and growth.

Similar to the value of dreams is the power of poetry. Poetry is used here, not in the narrower sense, but as the creation of meaning. This can happen when someone creates a poem or so embraces the poem of another as to make it one's own. But poetry may also take place in journaling or in the writing of fiction which creates a symbolic universe. The parables of Jesus are examples of stories which create meaning and which others can use and interpret to create meaning of their own. Seeing a movie, a theater production, or an MTV production can create meaning for the ones who appropriate the meaning, who make it their own. This is also true of a simple song which captures the love of two persons for each other and which continually recreates that love.

So reflection can take place in many ways. Some of the ones mentioned include dialogue, interactions with nature, interpreting dreams, and poetic acts as the creation of meaning.

Commitment

Reflection calls for action, decision making, wagering on the truth of the experience-expression-reflection. It calls for commitment and choice. How do these decisions and actions take place? They may take place as persons choose who they are becoming, choose this interpretation or that, choose this course of action or that.

Actions that continue signify commitment. This may be positive or negative. A woman who stays in a relationship where she is continually battered is in a committed relationship, but one that most likely should be broken. Ironically, each day she is wagering that things will get better. Symptomatic of the battering/battered syndrome is the belief that tomorrow will be different. On the other hand commitment may give courage to a woman to nurture her husband through a debilitating and terminal illness such as cancer.

Commitment may be confused with a misplaced view of responsibility. A woman in Latin America may continue commitment to her husband even though she knows he has several mistresses, even though he ignores her or refuses to speak to her. Is she in this context co-dependent in the sense of a co-dependent wife of an alcoholic husband who becomes an enabler of the disease? How does "commitment" become crooked or twisted?

Paul was committed to go to Damascus and arrest Christians as blasphemous. Only a dramatic conversion experience and years of reorientation enabled him to acknowledge his mistakes, and build a new commitment. How often do women find themselves in a commitment which should be changed? Reorientation usually requires a major shift, a new commitment, and all the pain which may go with that new commitment.

What are the challenges which women face around the world to examine their commitments, to acknowledge the truth of their experiences, to bring those experiences to expression, to reflect on the validity of those experiences/ expressions and then develop the courage to form those experiences/ expressions/

reflections into actions? And how can those actions develop into appropriate commitments?

Mother Teresa provides an example of how this unfolds. While she was teaching children of the middle class in India, she became aware of the overwhelming poverty of the large numbers of people who lived nearby. This experience over a continuing time period led her to express her concern, reflect on the process she was engaged in, and begin actions that led to a commitment to the poorest of the poor which became a lifetime global task.

Dorothy Day's experience of the poor in New York City led her to express her concern in many ways. That concern became action and lifetime commitment through writing, through starting a newspaper called *The Catholic Worker,* through starting a daily food program, and through establishing a house for the homeless. Consistency of her conscience and actions led her to become a pacifist even in the face of popular wars.

Such commitments can be contagious. That is partly why Mother Teresa's community has become worldwide, numbering in the thousands. In a parallel way, Dorothy Day's commitment has inspired thousands to follow her traditions and values in their own lives.

What about women facing famine in Africa? Commitment may mean basic survival, a daily struggle which may end in death. This is nevertheless commitment. This is action to "choose life" against overwhelming odds.

New Proclamation

After an original experience, an expression of that experience, the following reflection, and the action or commitment which follows, one always needs to return to the first naiveté, the simplicity of the first experience, the proclamation of the first insight. So the woman in Africa may find herself in a new situation with enough medical care and enough food to restore herself and her children to the normalcy of food as nourishment and as enjoyment.

The world was astonished when Nelson Mendela was finally freed after twenty-seven years in prison, and could move past bitterness or anger to the transcendence of a statesman and leader of his country. His experiences had found expression in multiple ways. These espressions led to reflection on those experiences and expressions. Out of these grew his actions and commitments. But he did not lose sight of his original vision. That vision was transformed by the intervening years so the person who emerged from prison was the same but in so many ways made new beyond the power of language.

In Mendela, in Mother Teresa, in Dorothy Day, we see persons who walk through the lifetimes of their continuing experiences, expressions, reflections, actions and commitments to a new place of joy, of simplicity, of the fullness of what a human life can be.

CHAPTER VIII:

HOW CAN COMMUNITY HELP US MOVE INTO THE FUTURE?

Chapter Eight:

How Can Community Help Us
Move into the Future?

The future is always the unknown. A first question for the future is community. What is the relationship between the one and the many? Feminism is one of the factors shaking up the perceived structures of relationships. At least theoretically in the earlier part of the twentieth century, the nuclear family was taken as the norm in some societies.[37] Male and female were assumed as the basic sexual partners and as the basic family unit. Sexual orientation within that construct was understood to be a given. Exceptions were outside societal expectations. Some individuals and some movements within feminism soon moved to include sexual and relational female partnering. Within another decade same-sex parenting became more widespread. By the end of the century many insurance companies and governments were accepting domestic partnerships as parallel with marriage. Same sex marriage ceremonies were being performed by some civil and religious authorities.

What is community? If we start with the one, we usually say one person is not a community. However, on the other hand, it is said that dinner conversation was never more stimulating than when Jefferson dined alone. In a religious community many persons living alone are perceived as anti-community. When a sociological value instrument was administered to those members living alone and to those members living in "community," the results revealed that those living alone were more "community-minded" than those who lived with others. Many living in families know that living at the same address, even having the same parents, does not make a community with shared values. If living at the same address makes a group torn apart, not speaking, and abusive, most would agree this is not a community, at least not a healthfully functioning community.

Does sexual union make a community? Many husbands and wives during the growth of feminism discovered the answer is no. Some husbands and fathers discovered their homosexual orientation. Some wives discovered themselves in love with female partners, felt obliged to leave their families and enter into relationship with their female partners. Their love included sexual relationships and sometimes the parenting of children either by adoption, by surrogate mothering, or by some other means.

Some feminists saw this new structuring of relationships as not necessary or as outside the boundaries of their feminist world views. They remained feminists within a male-female structure and often within a more traditional marriage. Perhaps male-female roles were rearranged to achieve more equity. Many governing bodies legislated what were intended to be more equitable marriage, property, and divorce laws. Sometimes these achieved more equity. Sometimes the results were not what was intended and injustice against women just took a different turn, in that some women were left without sufficient income. Some had supported their husbands through medical school, for example, and then found themselves divorced and left without schooling or income commensurate with their investment.

Some feminists now see themselves as living within a single way of life. Some indeed engage in "male bashing," but others simply choose to interact with other women, not to be involved with men, and to achieve an independence and freedom they do not see as a part of marriage. Some women recognize that they need to relate to some others for food and other basics of life, for certain services, for social interaction, but they consider themselves a "community" of one. They could not have grown into adulthood by themselves, but as adults, they can live what they consider healthful and fulfilling lives. In Western technological society, this has become possible. In most other world views, this is not acceptable. Women are expected to marry, to have children, and to assume whatever are the traditional roles. Abuse, being ostracized, being imprisoned, or even being killed are acceptable sanctions.

So questions about the present as well as about the future push us to ask new questions about community. **Who** are the persons who constitute a community? **What** are the relationships or bonds by which we recognize a community? **When** does a group become a community? What are the time elements of beginnings, developments, breakdowns and endings

of community? Or does a community end? What about place?
Is there a **Where** of community? Does residing in a place make
a community? If community members do not share a place, can
they continue as community? **Why** does a community form,
why does it grow, why does it break down? And **How** does all
this happen?

If we define community as a group of those who share
values, then the question today takes on new dimensions. With
chat rooms on the internet, with wireless phones that transcend
place, community may be developed with persons we have never
seen or with persons whose voices may come from San Francisco
or Boston or Atlanta. Gender may not even be identified.
Somewhat to their surprise some persons using e-mail without
identifying themselves in the more traditional way have found
more community and have even developed relationships which
have led to in-person meetings and in some cases marriage.

Support groups such as those found in Alcoholics
Anonymous may provide more community than traditional
marriage, family, or religious groups. A work group with
common goals and experiences may generate strong community.

The phenomenon of computer companies in the Silicon Valley often shows a bonding far stronger than that experienced in many families or in other traditional community groups.

So the question of <u>who</u> make up communities today is more complex than it used to be. On the other hand, diverse cultures continue to make clear that the western Victorian so called nuclear family is far from being universal. In western Asia, there is a group for whom the basic relationship model involves one woman and as many as seven men. Far from being oppressive, this often makes it possible for the woman to play one man against the other, to use her favors for control and as a means of obtaining what she wants. Some traditions of indigenous groups in Africa may include a king with four wives and "husband-wife" relationships. Some Mormon women in Utah complained mightily when their shared husband was arrested and jailed for polygamy. They felt their shared relationships worked well. In ancient Rome, male and female slaves, as well as other men and women, were available as sexual and even friendship partners.

These reflections lead us to explore the question of: <u>What are the relationships or bonds by which we recognize a</u>

community? Is the essence of community a sense of belonging? If so, what does it mean to belong? Some characteristics of belonging may include: origin or birth, allegiances or loyalties, places of residence, memberships, shared experiences, shared goals, shared relationships. But just as easily, any of these may produce a sense of alienation rather than belonging. For example, some adopted persons have a need to find their birth mothers or fathers, and when they do, they have a sense of belonging. This sense of alienation may even include siblings from the birth parents. Other adopted persons have such a strong sense of their adopted family, that they resist pursuing birth parents, and feel a sense of alienation from them even though they are unknown. If "belong" also connotes "property," in the sense that this book belongs to me, then belonging can have both positive and negative aspects. A maxim says that blood is stronger than other connections. For some this is a very positive feeling. A sense of belonging can transcend other values. On the other hand, some persons reject family precisely because they feel "owned" or oppressed by the required belonging.

Jean Vanier, the founder of l'Arche, writes about community out of lived experience with developmentally challenged persons. He relates an anecdote about Canadian indigenous children who have a strong sense of community. If a prize is offered for the first one to answer a question, the group work together to find the answer. It would be a violation for one to stand out from the rest. That one would lose solidarity.[38] This is in contrast to the dominant competitive values in western world views.

So origin or birth may or may not generate a positive sense of belonging. Another characteristic of the relationships by which we can recognize community are allegiances or loyalties. The root word is probably the same as that of ligament, that which binds. In Sicily, there is typically an assumed loyalty to the community which reminds us of tribal loyalties. The same is often true of Arab societies. The loyalties are deeper than place. They presume shared allegiance, whether the persons individually espouse shared values or not. Often the persons don't have a choice. The community is presumed to be far more important than individuals. Even in an individualist society like the United States, this phenomenon emerges frequently. After the terrorist attack 9/11/01, reactionary patriotism was so strong that groups or individuals who asked for alternative responses were perceived as unpatriotic. The "tribe" dominates to the exclusion of alternate allegiances. Even in sports, this kind of allegiance can squelch any alternate views. Sanctions can be so strong that even injury, death, or alienation can result. This aspect of community, allegiances or loyalties, can be inspiring, motivating, uplifting, but also can be oppressive, confining, and even death producing.

What about places of residence as characteristic of community? In times when persons lived their whole lives in a small town where most persons knew each other and where there was a shared history, place typically defined community. If the -mun root of community is related to "walls," that reminds us that towns were often circumscribed by walls to keep residents in and aliens out. This is even true now in the growing suburban "gated" communities of developed countries. In what we think of as a rather civilized modern world view, we still require passports, and assume the absoluteness of politically defined national boundaries. Second and third generation place of residence in the United States, and even citizenship, did not protect west coast persons of Japanese origin from being confined to detention camps in World War II. Wars and persecution propel persons from their places of residences to seek life in a better place. The astonishing migrations of the twentieth and twenty-first centuries attest to the vulnerability of place of residence as a primary characteristic of community.

What about memberships? Paul the New Testament apostle says we are members of one body. A member is a body part, a part of a whole, a constituent unit. The members of a physical body act as a whole. If one part is injured there are repercussions in all the parts. An injury to the foot may cause an ache in the head and a stomach upset. In fact, such symptoms may lead to diagnosis and even healing. The body can serve as model for community. The indigenous or modern awareness of the earth as community gives us another model. As we better understand the interaction of micro and macro earth communities, we are surprised at the interdependence and complexity of effects one part has on another part. Membership in a college or university community can generate a very strong sense of belonging. Although a person may graduate at age twenty-two, fifty years later loyalties can be even stronger. Membership in a country club or other social structure can supersede other allegiances. Such social structures can provide the basis for business, political, personal, and other relationships and weave the loyalties together in such a way that they overlap and add complexity of loyalties.

Shared experiences may construct one of the strongest senses of belonging. Military personnel in World War II often developed a deep connectedness that continued for fifty or sixty years. The elements of need, reliance, common training and goals, fear, courage, vulnerability can be knit within the physical-mental-emotional cells so as to produce a loyalty that often defies reason and other relationships. These qualities are recognized as integral to building group trust whether the training is for college leadership, a sales force, the forming of a religious community, the developing of a cult, or basic military training. Shared experiences form an underground network which is often not articulated, but which calls forth fierce and sometimes irrational loyalties.

Shared goals appear in a group of hockey or soccer ball players who start aiming for an Olympic spot. All other considerations take second place. The persons live, practice, and socialize together, often for twenty-four hours a day, seven days a week, until the goal is achieved. When the goal is achieved or lost, connections remain, but the community dissolves since it was held together primarily by the shared goal. Something similar can apply to a national or political group. If there is a common enemy, this can unite a group for a shared goal of defeating the enemy. This phenomenon appeared after the terrorist attack on the World Trade Buildings. War on terrorism became the slogan of a shared goal.

All of the above characteristics of belonging involve shared relationships. The relationship may involve connections recognized as superior/inferior, master/slave, friend/friend, parent/child, lover/lover, lover/beloved, oppressor/oppressed or others according to the complexity of human relationships. These may appear at the individual level, at a small group level, at a societal structural level, or at a regional or national level. So community and belonging have recognizable characteristics which cross structural boundaries.

After asking the question of the <u>who</u> and the <u>what</u>, we can ask the question of the <u>when</u>. What are the time elements of beginning, developments, breakdowns and endings of community? Or does a community end? Beginnings may take place in birth, in joining, in being inducted, or in exposure that leads to falling in love. A wanted baby is immediately perceived as belonging. Sometimes physical characteristics make this clear. She looks just like her mother. Groups celebrate the new addition. Perhaps churches hold welcoming ceremonies. Sometimes a baby is not wanted. The mother may reject the child, throw it away, or kill it. Far from seeing the child as belonging to her, even though it emerged from her body, she perceives it as alien. She does not accept the societal norm of belonging. Some feminists in pro-abortion groups have formulated political language that supports a woman in making a choice of rejecting that which was conceived. Such a position recognizes the perceived alien quality of that which was conceived.

What happens when we join a group? The time event changes not only relationships but persons. To join a military group may be seen as ontological. In a way, the one making the commitment becomes a different person. The loyalties, the responsibilities, the effects modify person and personality. In another context, resistance to or attraction to cults makes such changes. Sometimes we no longer recognize the person who has joined the cult. Education can bring about comparable differences, but often such differences are quite gradual and not recognized as easily.

Falling in love can be gradual, but sometimes it is instantaneous. A woman will say: As soon as I saw him, I knew this was the man I would marry. A man can say the same about a woman. They typically remember the moment, perhaps the song that was playing, perhaps the clothing the other was wearing. Time stands still or becomes cosmic.

So in community, there are beginnings, developments, breakdowns, and endings. Whether the context is birthing, joining, being inducted, or falling in love, in retrospect at least, we can often point to the beginnings. But we can also see developments over time, we can see crisis points and breakdowns, and sometimes sadly, we can see endings. Language helps us to name the temporalities and the qualities of those points in time.

Besides who, what, and when, we can ask: What is the where of community? Does community need a place? What effect do beginnings, developments, breakdowns, and endings have on community? Feminism has raised some new challenges in our thinking about community and place, but other changes in world views are also forging new ways of thinking. When two partners, whether heterosexual or homosexual, whether married or not, work in locations removed from each other, they have to work out how they will maintain separate residences, how they will get together, and how they will take care of separate and shared responsibilities. If children or other dependents are involved, sometimes the communities multiply. If relationships depend on the technology of e-mail, is the computer the place of community? Is this one reason some persons become addicted to the computer, spending a large amount of their time there? Multiple families or communities can require travel with concomitant expenses and time commitments. Some persons can find themselves feeling schizophrenic. Others opt out and renege on their responsibilities. Laws are increasing to try to require support for children from a parent who seeks to escape that responsibility.

Groups aiming to form community usually soon look for a place to make it easier. A youth group or a group of scouts look for their own place where they can meet. If a church is forming, a building may be rented at first, but plans usually start for a church of their own. If a young married couple live with their parents at first, one of their hopes is usually for a place of their own. In the breakdown of what had been perceived as traditional families or communities, we may not be surprised to learn of the large number of persons who live alone.

Why do people come together in community? The answer depends on how one defines community. Mary F. Rousseau in her study *Community: The Tie That Binds* distinguishes what she sees as real community from what she calls contract. For her the only real community is that identified with altruistic love which brings about a single good in common.

The key to love as a communion which heals our ontological loneliness, in a more realistic way than does cognition, is located right here. When I identify another's good as my own...The paradoxical reality of community, in which many become one without ceasing to be many, results from this process of identification.[39]

In contrast, according to Rousseau, a contract does not make a community. A contract is limited by time and space and works toward a "manageable synthesis."[40] Although the contract may involve perceived "friendships," the relationships are utilitarian or for pleasurable or egoistic effects, rather than the love described above.

If we take real community as involving altruistic love of the other, then it is possible to think of having community with all of humankind as well as with the neighbor who lives nearby. On the other hand, we may live with others and not have community in the fullest sense, or even in a basic sense. We can think of Gandhi or Mother Teresa as loving all of humankind and experiencing community with all human beings. However, a woman living with a man who abuses her, or a group sharing a common dwelling, may not be a community. In fact, they may be the opposite.

How does community take place? Anyone who has tried to build community knows how challenging this can be. A group of Christians lived together in the same house with strong commitment to building community. They were quite successful. Then a person was invited in and before long, things started to fall apart. The community was faced with a classic dilemma. If the person remained, it seemed the community would disintegrate. The members had tried over a period of time to address the concerns. They had made compromises. They had tried various strategies. They felt they were practicing love. But signs showed that even over time, the results were inadequate. It became clear that unless the person went elsewhere, the community would no longer exist. This was a contradiction of their assumptions but a reality they were dealing with. The decision was made to help the individual move, but all considered the process and end result the brokenness of the human condition.

So the <u>how</u> of community is always in process. We can define four stages in such a process. There is the beginning or primitive stage where a willing spirit and accompanying energy generates creativity and stamina. This is sometimes called the foundational series of events. As the group continues or grows, organization is needed and structures of organization are put in place. More often than not, the organizational structures become more important than the original spirit, and the third or bureaucratic stage sets in. But even at the organizational stage, there are usually members who recognize some loss of spirit and begin efforts to renew the spirit. So there will be new beginnings which will continue through the more dominant organizational and bureaucratic stages. In a fourth stage bureaucratic structures often break down of their own weight and the community enters into a process of dissolution. As long as there is renewal of the spirit, a community may often continue, transform itself, and free itself of some of the deadening characteristics. If the spirit is not renewed, the group can continue as though petrified or the group can dissolve. What makes possible one direction rather than another? It is challenging to sort it out. Some of the questions addressed above may suggest answers. But there are cultural, temporal, historical, and political reasons that are part of the process too. Results are not always easily predictable.

So feminism raises new questions for our understanding of community, of the problem of the one and the many. Reciprocally, other structures in society continue to raise questions for feminism. Mutual interaction or study can enlarge the views of each. As we move into the future, we move into the unknown. What structures we are affirming or changing are not always clear. Certainly the ramifications of those affirmations or changes are not clear. The questions examined here may help us to at least name what are some of the present challenges.

CHAPTER IX:

HOW CAN COMMUNICATION HELP US MOVE INTO THE FUTURE?

Chapter Nine:

How Can Communication Help Us
Move into the Future?

Moving into the future involves communication. Communication requires a sender of a message, the message, and the receiver of the message. In many fields of animal study, we have learned much in the last fifty years. Animal communication is far more sophisticated than we previously thought. Whales send messages and songs for long distances through the water. We can record a variety of their songs. We can detect patterns related to meeting, birthing, migration, and danger, but as receivers of their messages, humans are at a very early stage.

At least since classical times, dolphins have intrigued humans, not only with their intelligence, but with many other characteristics, including their playfulness and their interest in interacting with humans. Dolphins and whales apparently have high capacity to receive signals from the environment, including sound or other sensory experiences related to pollution or even to the anticipation of earthquakes. Scientists who work with these mammals are in awe at what they have learned, but they are even more in awe at what they do not know.

People who work with animals in the wild or even in a zoo are constantly challenged at the communication they witness. The sender-receiver codes have developed with the genes and grow with appropriate nurturing. Humans can observe and learn about a few behaviors to expect, but for the most part are outsiders. The migration patterns of elephants in the deserts of South Africa leave the aerial observer in awe as he watches them travel great miles to the water holes necessary for their existence.

Observers of domestic pets are surprised at what they sometimes call the intuition of their cats or dogs. There are communication systems outside the realm of human experience. Two house cats detected the fall in the bathroom during the night of an older sick woman in the house. The regular caregiver and "owner" of the cats was away. The substitute caregivers were sleeping behind a closed door. The cats were not only alert to the fall and the inability of the woman to get up or help herself, but they scratched on the closed door of the substitute caregivers until they were aroused to help.

Since it has been discovered that certain dogs can evidently anticipate seizures of their epileptic "owners," some dogs who have this ability have been trained to react to their perception and notify the epileptics so they can seek a safe position or get help.

Even insects have an astonishing power of communication. Generations of monarch butterflies communicate genetically and in other ways that scientists guess may be related to the magnetism of the earth or the position of the stars. Whatever the mysteries involve, for thousands of years monarchs have followed their processes of metamorphosis and migration that defy the human imagination.

Many persons have observed the astonishing dance and travels of honey bees which have powers of communication and knowledge that humans can only observe.

All such communication involves a sender, a receiver, an encoded message, and interpretation of the message. The sender, receiver, message, and interpretation operate within what humans call a worldview, a field of experience, or multiples of those worldviews, or of those fields of experience.

What can any of these insights tell us about the future and feminism? They can remind us of the long history of human female and male. A recent discovery of a "human" skull in Chad, Africa is dated to perhaps seven million years ago. The female figurines found in the Near East or Europe date to perhaps ten thousand years ago. Female and male belong to mammals, including chimps and humans. But a human "arriving" even seven million years ago in a fifteen billion year old universe is still a newcomer.

Even in a ten thousand year time line, what we know about female/male is very limited. Early male archeologists named the female figurines "fertility goddesses." That name is more suspect in recent studies. We can describe female/male roles in some societies of the last five thousand years, but the descriptions rest on shaky evidence for the most part, and on contemporary interpretations which are hampered by the limitations of backward projections and the limitations of contemporary worldviews.

How will the female evolve in the future? What directions will feminism take? And how will these affect communication? In Western society we can project an increase of single females as well as of lesbianism. In related worldviews, within the world of some single females or the world of lesbianism, senders, receivers, the encoded messages, and interpretations may exclude other worldviews and find "truth" only in their own experience. Such communication with groups will sharpen the gulf between themselves and others. Some opt for "diversity" or "inclusivity." But too often such a communication system is sociologically naive or blind to the depths of cultural world views.

From a planet perspective, lesbianism or women single by choice or default seem to affect relatively small numbers compared to world population. At the other extreme is the continuing lot of large numbers of women in the world who because of poverty or cultural bias, find themselves in a male dominated culture, in which they are subject to sexual and power

Loretta Dornisch

abuse. Whether they are among the millions of South African women who by force have contracted aids, and who die, leaving their children with or without aids, or whether they are Japanese women dependent on male patronage for jobs or marriage income and status, their positions can foresee freedom only in death or in conforming to the dominant worldview.

For those women not in the above world views, if they have enough hope, courage, and opportunities, they may be able to make new roles for themselves and perhaps for their children. As single parents they may improve the situation for themselves and those who follow. Migration to new lands, great vision, perseverance, and education are beacons for a new perception of feminism and of what women can be and do. Communication then depends on deliberate choice of new models of sender, receiver, encoded message, and interpretation. A woman fleeing from war in Somalia endured years of "indentured slavery" as an undocumented worker in a suburban California house, but eventually found freedom to become documented, married, autonomous, and free. Former systems of communication had to be rejected, and new ones formulated to make the transition possible.

Many women who choose divorce over what they consider oppression are refusing to continue to accept oppressive communication systems, are choosing to reject them, and enter into a new system of sender, receiver, message, interpretation that speaks a truth for them even though the obstacles are formidable. Some women through marriage counseling are able to achieve a comparable goal and stay with the marriage.

What does this mean for the future of women and of feminism? If most women are unable or unwilling to enter into a freedom of communication, the expectation is that the future will not be too different from the past. However, if enough women and men and the cultures of which they are part can recognize the power of communication systems, can evaluate them, and choose to reject, modify, or radically change them if necessary, the lives of women, men, and children and the possibilities of feminism can offer hope for a new kind of world.

END NOTES

[1]Zimmer cites as sources for overview Josephine Donovan, *Feminist Theory: The Intellectual Traditions of American Feminism* (New York: Continuum, 1991); Patricia Hill Collins, *Black Feminist thought: Knowledge, Consciousness, and the Politics of Empowerment* (London: HarperCollins Academic, 1990); Gisela Bock and Susan James, eds., *Beyond Equality and Difference: Citizenship, Feminist Politics and Female Subjectivity* (New York: Routledge, 1992). *In the Embrace of God: Feminist Approaches to Theological Anthropology*, ed. Ann O'Hara Graff. (Maryknoll. New York: Orbis. 1995).

[2]bell hooks, *Feminist Theory from Margin to Center.* (Boston: South End Press, 40) quoted in Graff as above.

[3]Graff, 66.

[4]*Ibid.*, 68. Quotation from Virginia Vargas Varela, *El Aporte de la Rebeldia de las Mujeres* (Lima, Peru: Flora Tristan, 1989), 144-145.

[5]Mary Ann Hinsdale in "Heeding the Voices" (22-48) in Graff (*op.cit.*) provides an excellent survey of some of the persons involved.

[6]A short version of these insights appeared in *New Catholic World*, "Experience as Life Story." Vol. 222 No 1328, March/April 1979, 58-61.

[7]Bernard Lonergan, *Method in Theology.* New York: Herder and Herder. 1972.

[8]An excellent volume offers insights from a number of perspectives on *Lonergan and Feminism*, edited by Cynthia S.W. Crysdale. Toronto: University of Toronto Press. 1994.

[9]Elizabeth Schussler Fiorenza, *In Memory of Her.* New York: Crossroad. 1985.

[10]Chung Hyun Kyung, *Struggle To Be the Sun Again.* Maryknoll, NY: Orbis, 1994.

[11]Lonergan, *op.cit.* 268.

[12]*Ibid.* 333.

[13]Paul Ricoeur, "Fatherhood: From Phantasm to Symbol," 468-497 in *Conflict of Interpretations.* ed. Don Ihde. Evanston: Northwestern University Press, 1974.

[14]See John L. McKenzie, "God," *Dictionary of the Bible*, Milwaukee: Bruce Publishing Company, 315-318, 1965.

[15]See note 1 above. Graff, ed.

[16]See Lonergan, 9.

[17]Lonergan, 344.

[18]*Ibid.* 351ff.

[19]*Ibid.* 355.

[20]*Ibid.* 356.

[21]Corley, Kathleen E, *Private Women Public Meals.* Peabody, MA: Hendrickson Publishers. 1993.

[22]Mk 6:14-29

[23]Mollenkott, Virginia Ramey, "An Evangelical Feminist Confronts the Goddess," *The Christian Century*, 20 October, 1982, 1040. References 22-25 are quoted in Ferm, Deane W. *Contemporary American Theologies.* San Francisco: HarperCollins. 1981, 1990.

[24]Gutierrez, Gustavo, *A Theology of Liberation.* Maryknoll, NY: Orbis, 1973, 1988.

[25]Wagner, C. Peter, *Latin American Theology: Radical or Evangelical? The Struggle for the Faith in a Young Church.* Grand Rapids, MI: Eerdmans, 1970, 24.

[26]Marty, Martin and Peerman, Dean eds. *New Theology No. 6.* New York: The Macmillan Co., 1969, 131-134.

[27]Torres, Sergio and Fabella, Virginia, eds. *The Emergent Gospel.* Maryknoll, NY: Orbis Books, 1976, 271.

[28]Soelle, Dorothee, *The Strength of the Weak: Towards a Christian Feminist Identity.* Philadelphia: The Westminster Press. 1984.

[29]Jurgen Moltmann, *The Crucified God.* New York: Harper & Row. 1974; *Experiences of God.* Philadelphia: Fortress Press. 1980; *The Power of the Powerless.* San Francisco: Harper & Row. 1983.

[30]*The Crucified God*, 270-272.

[31]*Ibid.,* 317-338.

[32]Akbar S. Ahmed, *Islam Today, A Short Introduction to the Muslim World.* London, New York: I.B. Tauris. 1999.

[33]*Ibid.,* 8.

[34]*Ibid.,* 10.

[35]*Ibid.*, 15.

[36]Mary Pat Fisher, *Religion in the Twenty-first Century*. Upper Saddle River, NJ: Prentice Hall, Inc. 1999. 47.

[37]Rosemary Radford Ruether, *Christianity and the Making of the Modern Family*. Boston: Beacon Press. 2000. Ruether's book is an outstanding study of the history and changing ideologies related to the construct of the family. Chapter headings include: The Making of the Victorian Family and The Many Faces of American Families in the Year 2000.

[38]Jean Vanier, *Community & Growth*. New York, NY: Paulist Press. 1976. 3. For this story Vanier cites Rene Lenoir. *Les Exclus*. Paris: Le Seuil. 1974.

[39]Mary F. Rousseau, *Community. The Tie That Binds*. Lanham, New York, London: University Press of America. 1991. 42.

[40] *Ibid.*, 19.

ABOUT THE AUTHOR

Loretta Dornisch, Ph.D. is professor of Religious Studies at Edgewood College, Madison, Wisconsin, where she incorporates new theories of interpretation in her courses. She is the author of *A Woman Reads the Gospel of Luke* (The Liturgical Press, 1996), *Paul and Third World Women Theologians* (The Liturgical Press, 1999), and *Faith and Philosophy in the Writings of Paul Ricoeur* (Mellen) and various articles. She can be reached at ldornisch@edgewood.edu.

Printed in the United States
57518LVS00003BA/133

KANSAS CITY
ROYALS

AL WEST

RICHARD RAMBECK

Published by Creative Education, Inc.

123 S. Broad Street, Mankato, Minnesota 56001

Art Director, Rita Marshall
Cover and title page design by Virginia Evans
Cover and title page illustration by Rob Day
Type set by FinalCopy Electronic Publishing
Book design by Rita Marshall

Photos by Tom Dipace, Duomo, National Baseball
Library, Michael Ponzini, Bruce Schwartzman,
Sports Illustrated, UPI/Bettmann, Ron Vesley and
Wide World Photos

Library of Congress Cataloging-in-Publication Data

Rambeck, Richard.

  Kansas City Royals / by Richard Rambeck.

  p.   cm.

  Summary: A team history of the Kansas City Royals,
born in 1969 and successful ever since.

  ISBN 0-88682-440-0

  1. Kansas City Royals (Baseball team)—History—
Juvenile literature.   [1. Kansas City Royals (Baseball
team)—History.   2. Baseball—History.]   I. Title.
GV875.K3R36 1991   91-10391
796.357'64'0978139—dc20   CIP

THE EARLY YEARS

Located practically in the center of the United States, Kansas City is the second-largest city in Missouri. Overlooking the majestic Missouri River, the city is on the western edge of the state, right on the Missouri/Kansas border. Kansas City is a thriving metropolis with almost 450,000 people.

A major freshwater port, Kansas City is also a hub and rail transportation. In addition, it is home to thirteen colleges and universities, an unusually high number for a city of its size. Kansas City also has a rich sports tradition, thanks to the Kansas City Chiefs of the National Football League and to a baseball team that has been one of the best in the major leagues over the past two decades.

An all-time Royal great, Freddie Patek.

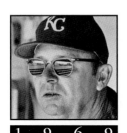

1 9 6 9

Led by manager Joe Gordon, the Royals won 69 games and finished in fourth place.

The Kansas City Royals, born in 1969 as an expansion team in the American League, have had kingly success, winning several division titles, two American League pennants, and one World Series championship in a little more than twenty years. The team, in fact, performed well from the beginning. The secret to Kansas City's success was a rich owner who vowed to make the Royals into champions.

THE ROYALS' ACADEMY OF SUCCESS

Ewing Kauffman paid $6 million to assume ownership of the Royals, but that was only his initial expense. Kauffman decided he would spend whatever it took to build the best minor-league system in baseball. He was convinced that was the only way for the Royals to succeed as an expansion team. His logic proved correct. The key to the Royals' success in developing quality young talent was the Kansas City Royals Baseball Academy, a kind of school for young players. Other major-league owners laughed at Kauffman's idea—at first. But the Baseball Academy would soon produce amazing results.

The idea was to find thirty of America's finest natural athletes—not necessarily baseball players—and teach them to play the game. The concept worked; in no time at all, the Academy's first graduating class was dominating other minor-league teams. Although the Academy was eventually closed down, it helped produce one of the finest minor-league systems in baseball. It also laid the foundation for the Royals' success throughout the 1970s and into the 1980s.

The sensational George Brett.

The amazing Royals posted a winning season (85–76) in 1971, which was only the third year of the team's existence. Kansas City, behind the talents of outfielders Amos Otis and Lou Pinella, wound up second in the American League's West Division, finishing behind the powerful Oakland A's. Unfortunately for the Royals, they were doomed to wind up behind the A's for the next five years. Oakland, a franchise that had once called Kansas City home, won five consecutive AL West titles from 1971 through 1975. The A's also won American League pennants and World Series championships in 1972, 1973, and 1974.

On July 9, shortstop Fred Patek became the first Royal to hit for the cycle.

BRETT THE GREAT MAKES A HIT

The Royals, meanwhile, were building a team around the talents of Amos Otis, first baseman John Mayberry, infielder Hal McRae, second baseman Frank White, and pitchers Dennis Leonard and Steve Busby. In addition to these fine players, the team had a burly third baseman named George Brett who batted .308 in 1975, which was only his second full season in the big leagues. He also led the American League in hits (195) and triples (thirteen) that season. As his teammates and the rest of the American League would soon discover, Brett would only get better.

Brett, a fun-loving sort, didn't let the pressure get to him. "George loves the game, it's that simple," said pitcher Andy Hassler, a longtime friend of Brett's. "He's out there to have fun. That eases a lot of the pressure. The best thing about him is that he doesn't take himself too seriously, not like a lot of superstars."

Brett may not have taken himself seriously, but opponents wondered if he was seriously strange. Opposing catchers claimed Brett talked to himself constantly while he was hitting. "Sometimes I think the catcher can hear me, but I try not to let him," Brett said. "I'll say, 'I'm hot,' or 'I'm really swinging the bat good,' or 'I'm going to hit this pitcher.' But, hey, that's where it ends. It's not like I'm always having conversations with myself. I mean, I don't go back to my hotel room and say, 'What do you want to watch on TV, George? Oh, I don't know. Johnny Carson looks pretty good tonight.'"

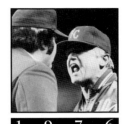

1 9 7 6

Whitey Herzog was named the AL Manager of the Year for leading the Royals to the division crown.

It was Brett and the Royals who looked pretty good in 1976. Led by second-year manager Whitey Herzog, the Royals finally aced out the A's and won the AL West title with a 90–72 record. Brett won the American League batting title with a .333 average. He also had 215 hits and fourteen triples. Hal McRae wound up second in the league in hitting, just one-thousandth of a point behind teammate Brett. In addition, Kansas City's pitching staff, led by Doug Bird, Paul Splittorff, Larry Gura, and Steve Busby, was one of the best in the American League.

In the American League Championship Series, the Royals fell behind the New York Yankees one game to none and then two games to one. Facing elimination in game four of the best-of-five series at fabled Yankee Stadium in New York, Kansas City scored three runs in the fifth inning to claim a 7–4 victory. In game five the Royals fell behind 6–3, but Brett's home run keyed a three-run eighth-inning rally to tie the game. In the bottom of the ninth, however, New York first baseman

Pitcher Mark Gubicza.

Frank White slides in safely.

Former Royal catcher and manager John Wathan (right) completed his second season with Kansas City.

Chris Chambliss hit a lead-off home run to give the Yankees the victory.

New York had the American League pennant, but the Royals had high hopes for the future. They lived up to most of those hopes by winning division titles in 1977 and 1978. But Kansas City came up short each year in the American League Championship Series against the New York Yankees.

WILSON STREAKS TO STARDOM

Even though the 1978 season ended in disappointment for the Royals, the future was brightened by the emergence of a new star, a fleet-footed outfielder named Willie Wilson. Wilson was the type of player the Royals used to produce out of their Baseball Academy.

He was a great athlete—one of the fastest humans alive, in fact—but not necessarily a great baseball player. "Wilson may be the fastest person I've seen in a uniform," Whitey Herzog claimed. "The whole thing with him is his bat. If he develops, he could be an awesome player."

Wilson, however, took a while to develop, mainly because the Royals insisted the right-handed hitter learn to switch-hit. "They called me up in '77 after winter ball in Puerto Rico, where I did terrible," Wilson recalled. "They said, 'We're gonna make you a switch-hitter.' It was pretty tough for me to turn around and hit a baseball from the other side at the age of twenty-two. That's something kids do when they're eight and nine years old. I disagreed with it at first, but they said, 'If you want to get to the majors, this is the best way to do it.'"

Actually, the Royals told Wilson he would never be a major-leaguer unless he either switch-hit or batted left-handed only. "Now I'm *glad* they asked me to do it," Wilson said. "Otherwise, I don't think I'd have made it to the majors this quick."

But Wilson struggled during the 1978 season, hitting only around .200. "I thought he'd chosen the wrong sport," said Brett, who watched in horror as Wilson swung wildly at pitches that were nowhere near the strike zone. "He was down on himself. He needed encouragement, confidence, and a lot of instruction." The Royals, however, were willing to give Wilson time to learn how to be a switch-hitter, especially because he could steal a base or two every time he got on. "When I get to first," Wilson said, "I figure second and third will be mine in just a second or two."

1 9 7 8

Second baseman Frank White won his second consecutive Gold Glove and was named to the AL All-Star team.

13

Center fielder Amos Otis established a club record with 10 putouts in a game against Texas.

Kansas City also loved Wilson's speed in the field. "He's just got an average arm, but I don't think anybody in the American League can go as far on a fly ball and catch it," said Jim Frey, who took over for Whitey Herzog in 1979 as Kansas City's manager.

Wilson improved dramatically in 1979, but the Royals dropped to second in the AL West behind the surprising California Angels. Jim Frey's first year as Royals manager was filled with injuries and disappointments. George Brett had a remarkable year—twenty-three home runs and 107 runs batted in—but he also missed several key games with aches and pains that resulted from surgery before the season. Hal McRae also missed some games because of off-season surgery.

The Royals, however, put it all together in 1980. Pitcher Dennis Leonard won twenty games, and Larry Gura added eighteen victories. Willie Wilson hit .326, and John Wathan batted .305 while splitting time between catching and playing the outfield and first base. Meanwhile, regular first baseman Willie Mays Aikens smacked twenty home runs and drove in ninety-eight runs. But nobody—nobody—in baseball had a better year in 1980 than George Brett. He hit .390, the highest batting average in the majors since Boston Red Sox star Ted Williams posted a .406 mark in 1941.

Brett actually didn't start the 1980 season very well, hitting only .247 in the middle of May. But he was a notoriously slow starter at the plate. By July he had raised his average to .337. Then he really got hot. For the rest of the season, he batted .421. From July 18 to August 18, he put together a thirty-game hitting streak. On August 17 his average jumped over .400 for the first time. Nine

14   *Ex-Royal Bo Jackson.*

For the second time in his career Hal McRae was named the Designated Hitter of the Year.

days later Brett was batting .407, and he was hitting above .400 as late as September 19. Brett did all this in spite of missing forty-four games because of injuries.

"We all come here with talent," Hal McRae said. "But the stars are the ones who don't have to work at concentrating. The superstars are the ones who are unconscious. They're in a trance. That's what George was in. I've been there, too, but not for as long. You can actually visualize the line drive jumping off your bat when you're still kneeling in the on-deck circle."

Thanks to Brett, the Royals jumped back to the top of the AL West. They won their fourth division title in five years and then faced the New York Yankees in the American League Championship Series. This time Kansas City would not be denied the pennant. The Royals won the first two games in Kansas City, and then trailed 2–1 in the seventh inning of game three. After a double by Wilson and an infield single by shortstop U.L. Washington, Brett stepped to the plate to face New York ace relief pitcher Rich "Goose" Gossage. Brett looked out at Gossage and began talking to himself. "You're hot," he told himself. "This guy can't get you out."

Gossage didn't; Brett slammed his first pitch into the third tier of seats beyond the right-field fence. The Royals had a 4–2 lead, and their ace reliever, Dan Quisenberry, closed the door on the Yankees, giving Kansas City a three-game sweep and a spot in the World Series for the first time in franchise history.

In the World Series, the Royals split the first four games with the Philadelphia Phillies and had a 3–2 lead in the ninth inning of game five. But the Phillies, behind series Most Valuable Player Mike Schmidt, rallied for a

Hal McRae.

The lightning-quick Willie Wilson.

For the first of four consecutive seasons closer Dan Quisenberry led the AL in saves.

4–3 victory. The series headed back to Philadelphia with the Royals just one game from elimination. Philadelphia, sensing the kill, scored two runs in the third inning and never gave up the lead, winning 4–1.

After winning the American League pennant in 1980, the Kansas City franchise underwent a lot of turmoil in the next few years. First, Dick Howser replaced Jim Frey as manager midway through the 1981 season. The following year, the experts looked at the aging Royals and picked the team to finish fourth, which was lower in the standings than Kansas City had been in a long time. But the Royals veterans responded. Hal McRae wound up leading the league in RBI with 133. Willie Wilson won the American League batting title with a .332 average and also topped the league in triples with fifteen. Additionally, Dan Quisenberry outdistanced all American

League relief pitchers with thirty-five saves. The Royals finished second in the division to the California Angels, which was considered excellent for a team that was thought to be over the hill. In 1983, however, the news would not be so good.

Midway through the 1983 season, four Royals—including long-time stars Willie Wilson and Willie Mays Aikens—were arrested on drug charges. For weeks the headlines in the sports section told of turmoil and court dates, not victory and teamwork. The Royals' season, and their sense of family, was ruined. Howser faced having to rebuild not only the team's aging pitching staff, but the club's morale as well. Amazingly, the Royals managed to accomplish both with one approach: giving expanded roles to young, enthusiastic players, particularly pitcher Bret Saberhagen.

Dan Quisenberry shattered the major league record of 38 saves by finishing with 45 for the year.

SABERHAGEN SPARKS THE ROYALS TO NEW HEIGHTS

The Royals, an exciting combination of young and veteran players, surprised everyone by winning the AL West title in 1984. Although they were swept in the American League Championship Series by Detroit, Kansas City players knew they had had a remarkable year. The next season was even more remarkable. The main difference in 1985 was the performance of Saberhagen, who was only twenty-one but who pitched like a seasoned veteran. Saberhagen led a late-season comeback that gave the Royals the division title. He posted a 20–6 record and was honored with the American League's Cy Young Award. Kansas City engineered another comeback in the American League

Bret Saberhagen.

Championship Series against Toronto. The Royals fell behind three games to one, but then rallied to win three straight and claim their second American League pennant.

The experts gave the Royals no chance to defeat cross-state rival St. Louis in the World Series. The Cardinals, after all, had won 101 games, the most in major-league baseball. So no one was really surprised when St. Louis won the first two games in Kansas City to take a commanding lead. The Royals then fell behind three games to one, just as they had against Toronto, and were just one game from winding up second-best again. But this time it didn't happen. Kansas City won game five, and then staged a late rally to claim game six and tie the series 3–3. Saberhagen was the starting pitcher in game seven. Despite his youth Saberhagen had been Mr. Clutch all year, pitching superbly when the Royals truly needed a victory.

When he took the mound for the deciding game of the World Series, Saberhagen was nervous, but confident. He was also almost unhittable. "They couldn't catch up to his fastball," claimed Kansas City catcher Jim Sundberg. "He's like Catfish Hunter—you have to get him in the first couple of innings, or you're not going to get him at all." The Cardinals didn't get him at all. Saberhagen threw a complete-game shutout as the Royals rolled to an 11–0 victory. As St. Louis meekly went down in the top of the ninth, the Kansas City veterans couldn't wait to celebrate their first world title. Many of them were even screaming at Saberhagen to hurry up and end it. "It wasn't just a matter of waiting all year for this moment," Saberhagen said. "Some of those guys had been waiting

1 9 8 5

Bret Saberhagen capped off an unbelievable year by being named the World Series' Most Valuable player.

23

24   *Left to right: George Brett, Mark Gubicza, Bret Saberhagen, Willie Mays Aiken.*

for a championship for twelve, thirteen years. Hal McRae, Frank White—they wanted the last out to hurry up and get there."

When the last out did come, veterans such as George Brett, Frank White, and Jim Sundberg raced to hug the youngest Royal and the World Series Most Valuable Player—Bret Saberhagen. "I've never seen a better young pitcher," said St. Louis manager Whitey Herzog, the former Royals skipper. "He's phenomenal. [New York Mets pitcher Dwight] Gooden is more overpowering, but when he gets behind 2–0 [in the count], Gooden's going to come at you with the fastball. This kid can surprise you. He got a couple of strikeouts on change-ups that I would never have thought possible for someone so young."

Royals' manager Dick Howser led the AL to a rare All-Star Game victory.

BO JUST DOES IT ON THE BASEBALL FIELD

Thanks to Saberhagen's clutch performance, Kansas City finally had its championship. But in the years that followed, the Royals had to find a way to replace a lot of veteran players who were nearing the ends of their careers. The rebuilding process was hampered by injuries to George Brett and Saberhagen, who struggled to a 7–12 record in 1986. But Kansas City's youth movement got a major boost in 1986 when Bo Jackson, who had just won the Heisman Trophy, given to college football's best player, decided to play pro baseball instead of pro football. Although Jackson would later elect to try pro football as a "hobby," he maintains his first love is baseball. It isn't hard to see why. The six-foot-one, 225-pound Jackson has the physique of a bodybuilder and

Bo Jackson became the first 25–25 player in Royals' history, belting 25 homers and stealing 27 bases.

the strength of a weightlifter. He doesn't just hit the ball; he almost puts it into orbit.

"Players from both teams watch when Bo takes batting practice," Saberhagen said. "There's always the feeling that you're going to see something you never saw before, and we don't want to miss it." Players from all over the American League were talking about Jackson, who made his major-league debut in 1986 and became a full-time starter in the outfield in 1987. "Bo and [Jose] Canseco are the two guys that everybody wants to watch," remarked Seattle Mariners catcher Scott Bradley. "When they get done [with batting practice], you go into the clubhouse and swap stories about balls they hit. It doesn't matter if we haven't played the Royals for two months; Bo still gets talked about. Everyone has to have a topper Bo story."

Jackson, who is a left fielder and has sprinter's speed, not only knows how to hit long balls, he also knows how to play the outfield. "No matter how fast we're running toward one another after a fly ball, he seems to know where I am at all times," said Willie Wilson, who plays next to Jackson in center field. "Bo's the only out-fielder with whom I've never had a collision—thank God. Bo is the only baseball player that you sense can do whatever he wants. And you can't wait to see him do it." John Wathan, who took over as manager during the 1988 season, is amazed at Jackson's ability to make up almost instantaneously for what seems like an error. "You define mistakes differently with Bo," Wathan asserted, "because a mistake to a normal player isn't a mistake to Bo. He can outrun and outthrow mistakes."

Jackson also can outpower just about every player in baseball. He finished the 1989 season with thirty-two

1 9 9 0

NL Cy Young Award winner Mark Davis (left), was signed as a free agent during the off-season.

homers and 105 RBI. He also stole twenty-six bases. Yet, despite Jackson's heroics, the Royals have been unable to recapture their glory days. The team finished second in the AL West to the Oakland A's in 1989 and was picked by many experts to unseat the powerful A's in 1990. But the Royals collapsed. Saberhagen, who won the 1989 American League Cy Young Award, was haunted all season by injuries and poor run support. Meanwhile, Mark Davis, another recent Cy Young winner, was just haunted—period.

Davis won the 1989 National League Cy Young Award while with San Diego and then signed with Kansas City as a free agent. He promised to be the relief pitcher the Royals so desperately needed. Davis started the season as the team's stopper, but he blew several save opportunities and lost his confidence. The Royals,

Pitcher Tom Gordon.

Outfielder Danny Tartabull.

meanwhile, blew any chance they had of contending for the division title.

Despite the disappointment of 1990, the team is optimistic about the future. Infielders Kurt Stillwell and Kevin Seitzer, and outfielder Danny Tartabull are the keys to Kansas City's offense, although George Brett and Willie Wilson are still contributing. The pitching staff is ably manned by Bret Saberhagen, Mark Gubicza, and Tom "Flash" Gordon.

With these talented players, it's not hard to see why the Kansas City management is expecting to add to its impressive total of seven American League West Division championships. The Royals, who haven't won a title of any sort since the 1985 World Series, believe they have the ingredients to rise to the top. But then, the team has expected—and often met with—success since the day it was founded.